"Joe Bullock has elevated the mun
a sport no one in his right mind sho
to his protagonist, senior citizen Jc
most delightful possible way. My face smiled a lot as my brain immersed in Joe's
journey to—and through—the final round of The Masters."

—Mark Medoff, Oscar-nominated playwright, screenwriter,
film and theatre director. Tony Award, Oliver Award, Obie
Award, and Writers Guild of America Award recipient.

"This inspirational and unique story touches every golfer's heart. We know
we have a big God, but do we dream big enough to prove it to the world and to
ourselves? Do we trust our God enough to accomplish the things He wants us
to? A truly captivating read and engaging story."

—Bernhard Langer, two-time Masters Champion, former
number one ranked player in the world

"I love God and golf; if you do too, you won't want to miss *Walking with Herb*.
Thank you, Joe, for a wonderful guide for living."

—Ken Blanchard, author of *The One Minute Manager*

"Joe Bullock's *Walking with Herb* is a book for golf lovers who also aren't afraid
to consider the question of how God enters the events of our lives and makes
Himself known to us. You'll laugh a lot, reflect even more, and maybe end up
praying."

—Jeff Hopper, author of *Go for the Green* and editor of the Links Daily Devotional

"I found the book full of life lessons and golf lessons. Sometimes God is talking
to us and we just have to listen."

—Hal Sutton, former United States Ryder Cup Captain:

"Joe Bullock has managed to use humor and the great game of golf to weave
a beautiful faith message in *Walking with Herb*. This book will put a great big
smile on your face!"

—Bill Rogers, 1981 British Open Champion, former PGA Player of the Year

"Here comes a great 'shot' right on line to show the joy of grace and faith.
What a wonderful read about a most difficult subject, and truly difficult sport.
I honestly could not put the book down without finishing a beautiful example
of God's power."

—Charley Johnson, former all-pro quarterback for Denver, St. Louis and Houston

"Within these pages you will find fiction interlaced with fact, subtle humor and a golfer's fantasy fulfilled, skillfully enriched with an overriding spiritual theme. It is an interesting, thoroughly enjoyable book, penned by my friend who is no 'ordinary Joe'. "

—Lou Henson, Hall of Fame college basketball coach, who led two different programs (New Mexico State & Illinois) to the Final Four

"The most informative book on golf I have ever read. Should be part of a teaching manual. A book on golf that would be number one in any golf library."

—Guy Wimberly, member of Professional Golf Association Hall of Fame

"This book is part of the golf story that is not told enough. It is a must read for all golfers."

—Bill Eschenbrenner, 2005 National PGA Professional of the Year

"Joe Bullock's book, *Walking with Herb,* will take you down a pathway loaded with solid advice on living life properly and enjoying each step of the journey."

—Dale Brown, Louisiana State University Basketball Coach, member of National Collegiate Basketball Hall of Fame.

"In these pages Joe Bullock has created a fascinating blend of sports story, humor, and theological reflection. The author moves effortlessly between light-heartedness and serious discussion of religious questions. Bullock's novel will appeal to golfers and non-golfers alike, as well as readers who consider themselves believers or SBNR (spiritual but not religious !). I recommend this book as a source of encouragement for thoughtful people who like to cheer for the underdog and who just might want to make a difference in the world, however small."

—The Reverend Dr. Jeanne Lutz, Priest-In-Charge, St. Christopher's Episcopal Church, El Paso, Texas.

"In Joe Bullock's novel 'Walking with Herb", I was pleased to find out that God cares about golf. Over the years of my golfing adventures and misadventures I had become convinced that God didn't like golf at all, and didn't appreciate me playing it. Mr. Bullock's book adjusted my mistaken point of view. God loves me and is invested in what I am doing and how I am doing it. His love is constant, mine is sporadic. The lesson is ongoing in the novel as it is in life, and filled with wonder and faith in the face of obstacles. There is a 'Herb' out there for all of us, and Joe was fortunate to find him. I loved the book and like golf a little more."

—Craig T. Nelson, Emmy winning actor and producer.

WALKING
WITH HERB

A SPIRITUAL GOLFING JOURNEY TO THE MASTERS

JOE S. BULLOCK

WALKING WITH HERB
A SPIRITUAL GOLFING JOURNEY TO THE MASTERS

This is a work of fiction. All characters, names, incidents, organizations, and dialogue in this novel are either the products of the author's imagination or are used fictitiously.

iUniverse Star
an iUniverse LLC imprint

iUniverse books may be ordered through booksellers or by contacting:

iUniverse
1663 Liberty Drive
Bloomington, IN 47403
www.iuniverse.com
1-800-Authors (1-800-288-4677)

Because of the dynamic nature of the Internet, any web addresses or links contained in this book may have changed since publication and may no longer be valid. The views expressed in this work are solely those of the author and do not necessarily reflect the views of the publisher, and the publisher hereby disclaims any responsibility for them.

Any people depicted in stock imagery provided by Thinkstock are models, and such images are being used for illustrative purposes only.
Certain stock imagery © Thinkstock.

ISBN: 978-1-4917-9803-4 (sc)
ISBN: 978-1-4917-9816-4 (hc)
ISBN: 978-1-4917-9804-1 (e)

Library of Congress Control Number: 2016908256

Print information available on the last page.

iUniverse rev. date: 05/19/2016

FOR SHEILA, MY LOVING WIFE

ACKNOWLEDGMENTS

It's easy to find parallels between Joe Goodman's mission and my own. I probably had about as much business thinking I could write a book as Joe did thinking he could win the Masters. We both had a lot of help.

I would particularly like to recognize and thank all the good people at iUniverse. It wasn't easy guiding a rookie writer through a first book.

None of this would have happened without the encouragement of Jerry Tarde and Michael O'Malley at *Golf Digest* magazine. They took a chance and published an article I wrote about my father, "Dad's Last Shot," in the June 2011 edition of their magazine. I had never attempted to write anything for publication. Their positive evaluation of my work gave me the inspiration to try going to another level.

Much appreciation to Jeff Hopper and Jim Sheard for their help, as well as to Mark Medoff for a crash course in creative writing.

I also want to thank Sheila, my loving wife of thirty-two years. She supported me through the writing process from start to finish, putting up with my ups and downs as I struggled to get the story just right.

PROLOGUE

‖‖‖

FIRST TEE AT AUGUSTA NATIONAL GOLF CLUB, AUGUSTA, GEORGIA

The throng of spectators surrounding the first tee grew quiet as the official starter took his position between the markers. Taking a deep breath, he stood straight and tall and said, "Fore, please! Ladies and gentlemen, Joe Goodman now driving!"

My knees felt weak, and I could literally hear my heart beating in my ears. The announcer was talking about *me*! My heart sounded even louder, if that was possible: *thrum, beat, thrum, beat, thrum!*

Oh God, I think I'm going to be sick! I thought.

As I heard a polite smattering of applause, I tried to calm myself down while I teed my ball slightly behind the markers and went through my preshot routine. Teeing off near the lead for the fourth and final round of the Masters golf tournament is about as intense as it gets in the world of golf. As one of the four major professional golf tournaments, the Masters is among the most popular and well-viewed sporting events on the planet. With thousands of fans on-site and millions more watching me on television, it was understandable that I was a bundle of nerves. Yet I was also filled with a calm self-assurance derived from countless hours of brain training and just as many, if not more, hours of simply believing I was meant to prove that potential can be realized if you just have enough faith to get up off the couch and stop being an unloaded baked potato.

I set up to hit my opening drive, my confidence building. I felt sweat prickle on my forehead and wet my underarms. Playing in the next-to-last group, four strokes behind the coleaders, my caddy and I were perhaps the only people in the golfing world who thought I had a chance of winning, and even we weren't sure. Given the events of the last year, we believed winning was possible, provided my faith remained strong. At this point, even my faith was a bit twitchy, but I wasn't about to give up. No way.

I focused on completing a backswing as far as my sixty-three-year-old body would allow and swatted the ball down the middle of the fairway. More polite applause. Apparently a modest poke of about 255 yards did not merit a raucous "You da man!" from easily impressed fans. No big deal. I had hoped my effort would at least coax a "You da geezer!" from someone, but this was the Masters, not the Milwaukee Open. Fans here exhibited total decorum. They were expected to. Masters officials are highly offended by references to their galleries as "crowds," preferring the more genteel term of "patrons."

The starter resumed his position, cleared his throat, and introduced my playing companion: "Fore, please! Ladies and gentlemen, Billy Dale Rankin now driving!"

It would be hard to imagine a bigger difference between two competitors. Billy Dale, a young PGA touring pro from Texas, epitomized the modern professional golfer. Young, tall, and athletic, he oozed poise and confidence from every pore. Most of his life had been spent preparing for this moment. He had all the credentials to be the next Masters champion. Average-size and balding, I, on the other hand, looked to be somewhere between middle-aged and aged. A year or so earlier, before a momentous event yanked me from a rather mundane and dull existence as a banker in a small town, I had been desperately out of physical and spiritual shape. I'd pretty much stopped playing golf, a game I had once been passionate about and had even played competitively in college and in later years. Any confidence or poise I exhibited now was mostly faked for the cameras. It was a front, a sort of show put on for outside observers I figured would rejoice in seeing me fall flat on my wrinkled face.

Billy Dale teed his ball on the right side of the box and hit a perfectly shaped fade down the middle. His ball worked its way around the dogleg, rolling to a stop at least sixty yards past my ball. The gallery reacted enthusiastically, as though they were witnessing the emergence of the second coming of Jack Nicklaus. Herb, my caddy, coach, and spiritual guide, marched with me down the immaculate, almost unnaturally green fairway. Being close to the end of our mission, I felt a mixture of excitement and relief, along with my nerves. I knew I would have to call upon everything I had learned during the past year to stay focused and confident. Most importantly, despite the wildly improbable circumstances, I had to maintain an unshakable belief that this particular match at this particular time was bigger than I was. As the one in charge of my head and my game, Herb had his work cut out for him.

CHAPTER 1

||||||||||||||||||||||||||||||||||||||||||||||||||||||||||||||||||||||||||||||||||||||||||||||||||||||||||||||||||||||||||||||||||||||||||||||||||||||||

SOMETIMES LIFE CAN SURPRISE YOU. AND SOMETIMES IT JUST drags on without giving you anything very special to say about it. As the years passed, separating me from my boring youth by wider gaps, my hair went gray, thinned, and eventually went somewhere else, like on a never-ending all-inclusive vacation to Nassau. Nothing much in my background distinguished me from other relatively well-adjusted middle-class guys, the sort with pocket protectors, plastic-rimmed glasses, and suits you buy at Target. I'd spent most of my life in the same small town where I was born. Most of the roughly ten thousand residents were multigenerational agricultural folks, with deep roots and pride in their little community.

My love of golf started with my dad. Dad was the best golfer at our small country club's nine-hole course. He passed along enough talent for me to obtain a golf scholarship at the state university, where I quickly learned that my small-town golfing skills did not match Division I expectations. Most of the guys I was competing against had plans for pursuing careers as tour players or becoming club professionals. I was mediocre, at best, in the major college golf arena. I determined my time would be better spent working a part-time job and concentrating on my studies. Looking back on it, I suppose the decision was a good one, but it did chart a course to a life of stability with little risk of accomplishing anything memorable.

I found a job as a part-time teller at a local bank, where my supervisor was able to juggle my hours to accommodate my ever-changing class schedule. The flexible schedule allowed me to stay employed throughout my junior and senior years. After graduation, I was offered a job at a bank in my hometown. I loved small-town life and welcomed the chance to return to my roots. Like I said, big dreams and big accomplishments were things other people had and did. I was fine just being an average Joe, if you'll forgive the pun.

As a bachelor with lots of time on my hands, I had great potential for becoming a golf bum. Fortunately, I was smart enough to listen to the best advice anyone had ever given me. It came from an old family friend, Cliff Baldridge, who often sat by my family at church. Cliff told me, "You can be the best golfer in the county, as well as the most successful banker in town, but if you don't get married and have a family, you will be a damned failure."

Soon afterward, my high school sweetheart, Sheila, moved back to town. We started dating and married a few months later. She was Catholic. I was a Methodist. We embraced both churches, attending each on alternate Sundays. We settled in for the long haul, enjoying the relaxed pace of life in a rural environment, as well as the satisfaction inherent to lifelong relationships. We waited several years to have children. As a result of our late start, our kids were the age of our friends' grandchildren.

As time passed, my responsibilities at the bank increased. The majority of the stock in the bank was still controlled by the heirs of the original founding family. Wallace Matthews had started the bank on a shoestring in 1939, not a very auspicious time in terms of the American economy. The effects of the Great Depression were still powerfully entrenched, but World War II jolted our town, along with the rest of the country, right out of the economic doldrums into one of the bloodiest conflicts in history. The bank prospered in the postwar years.

When I arrived at the bank fresh out of college, the institution was being managed by the founder's grandson, Wallace Matthews III, better known around town as Wally. None of Wally's offspring had any interest in the business. He took it upon himself to groom me as his one-man succession plan. He was a golfing buddy of Dad's and had always thought highly of our family. Wally finally got tired of fighting the regulators and retired, handing the reins over to me about fifteen years ago, in my twenty-fifth year at the bank. He advised me to always remember that the bank and the town were, for all practical purposes, long-term partners in each other's success. "This bank won't survive if we don't help our customers survive" was his mantra. I agreed with the sentiment.

Small community banks are much different from large Wall Street banks, which are so justifiably vilified by the press. Community bankers live among their customers; they see them daily at the grocery store, in church, at PTA meetings, and so on. These small banks survive by supporting their communities, doing everything from helping local businesses survive to sponsoring the local Little League teams. Community bankers wouldn't dream of Wall Street shenanigans, such as taking a government bailout and then using it to pay themselves six-figure bonuses. My annual bonus always came out of the bank's modest profits and was barely sufficient to buy Christmas presents for my wife and kids. Most people think all bankers are wealthy. They're not.

Until the second week of April last year, a year before I found myself at Augusta, my life was unfolding in a reasonably satisfying, somewhat predictable pattern. And that was fine with me. That's the way I liked it. Sheila and I were enjoying the thirtieth year of a great marriage, the kids were out of college, and I was gearing up for retirement. But while you're making other plans, life can throw you a curveball that changes everything. I really should have seen it coming, but I didn't. I had no warning about how suddenly my life was about to explode from the comfortable box I'd built.

The event occurred on a typical Monday at my office, following a weekend I had spent in my den glued to the television broadcast of the Masters with friends. This gathering of friends at my house on Masters Sunday had become a regular spring ritual. Watching the Masters usually stirred up a resolve to get the clubs out and begin practicing for the upcoming season. In recent years, this familiar resolve had been trampled by other priorities since the spring planting season required me to devote most of my time to helping my farmer customers.

I was sitting at my desk, hoping the caffeine jolt from my second cup of coffee would provide the energy to help me complete a couple of senseless government-required monitoring reports. Both were designed to prove my bank wasn't engaged in any discriminatory practices. The government regulators don't seem to understand the community banking business model. Community banks do business where their bankers live. Community banks have to depend on repeat business, continually serving the same customers. They can't afford to be discriminatory. In a small town, your reputation for fairness is everything.

The caffeine kicked in. I booted up my computer and resolved to get the senseless reports done by noon. At that moment, the monitor started shaking violently. *Oh crud*, I thought, *I'll have to call the young nerds from IT to fix this darn thing. Probably keep me from getting these reports done by my self-imposed deadline.*

The monitor stopped shaking just as I reached for my intercom. The screen came to life, a blank window opened, and large, bold letters slowly started to form. I sat there just staring at the screen. I rubbed my eyes to make sure I was seeing straight.

"What the—" I blinked my eyes rapidly, in an attempt to clear my head. "Was there something in my coffee besides caffeine?" I said quietly. Rubbing my eyes again, I focused on the screen, not believing what I was seeing. It was still there. Bold letters stretched across my monitor.

"Hello, Joe. This is God! I have chosen you for a special mission. Please respond!"

Oh yeah, I thought, *I get it. This is a trick from one of my kids.*

It would be just like either Catherine, our oldest child, or her brother Todd to come up with something like this. They must be in cahoots with their friends in our IT department, I figured. They had managed to somehow hack into this thing, so that they could mess with what little mind I had left. This stunt was just like one of them. Although their mother and I had dutifully taken them to church, insisted on mealtime prayers, and taught Sunday school, our faith had never sprouted in our kids. They were good citizens but rarely attended church. They believed religious people of my generation weren't as far down the evolutionary path as their younger generation.

Okay, I thought, *I might as well bite the bullet and play along with this—at least show them the old man's sense of humor is still intact.* I typed, "It's about time I heard from you after all these years! I thought my mission was to work myself to death raising a couple of ingrates and then get back at them by squandering their inheritance."

> *"I knew this would be hard for you to believe. Turn around and look at your printer."*

I turned around to face the printer on my credenza. A sheet of paper popped out, with big, gold-colored letters:

> *"Behold and believe, Joe!"*

That was a pretty good trick, I had to admit, considering this printer printed only in black. The nerds in IT hadn't wanted to waste an expensive color printer on their technologically challenged boss.

Starting to become very unsettled, I typed back, "How did you do that?"

> *"Oh ye of little faith! All of your life, you have been told I can do anything. I suppose I could have done the burning bush thing again, but all the plants in your office are artificial, which would result in a melted sticky mess. I'll give you a more traditional sign. A white dove will land*

*on the branch just outside your window, wink at you,
and fly away. Look outside!"*

Still playing along, I swiveled my chair over to the window. Sure
enough, a white dove landed on a branch, winked at me, and quickly
flew away. I'm not the smartest guy on the block, but I knew I was in
over my head, on overload. I was like a 110-volt appliance plugged
into a 220-volt outlet.

Buying time, I spun around and typed, "Can you excuse me for
a minute? If I don't get to the restroom really fast, I am going to have
a rather ugly accident." It was part ploy and part reality. I did need to
get to the bathroom quickly.

"Sure, but hurry back—we've got some ground to cover."

I hurried to the bathroom. Thankfully, it was unoccupied. After
taking care of my near accident, I examined myself in the mirror: no
indications of abnormality, other than a rapidly increasing heart rate
and heavy breathing issues. I slapped myself on the side of my head
a couple of times. This technique had often fixed my television when
it was on the fritz; maybe it would resolve an issue with some sort of
loose connection in my brain. Had that really just happened? The chat
dialogue could very well be the work of some trick-playing hacker, but
the dove? Maybe I had just imagined the dove. I wanted to believe this
was real, but a healthy dose of cautious skepticism made sense.

I returned to my office, where I found a stack of paper in the
printer tray. I picked up the pages and was surprised to find the
government reports had been miraculously completed in my short
absence. Reaching for my keyboard, I typed, "Did you do these?"

*"Yes, and believe me, I dislike this regulatory nonsense as
much as you do. Any waste of time is an abuse of one of
my gifts to humankind. I did the reports because I want*

you to be free to concentrate. I am enlisting your help
for an important mission. Your life is about to change!"

My head was spinning. I was still questioning whether this entire thing was a joke, but the dove and now the reports were starting to make me a true believer in the improbable. Besides, I wanted to believe! I found myself really wanting to believe that God was talking directly to me. You don't have to be insane to think God talks to you. He talks to us all. I knew that. It's just that He'd never been so obvious about it.

"Help?" I typed, my fingers flying. "How can an ordinary guy like me be of help to you? Are you sure you've got the right guy? I've never done anything extraordinary in my entire life. My job, community involvement, and family responsibilities have me running around half-crazy most of the time. It's a wonder I haven't had a heart attack already. How could I take on anything else?"

"Don't take this wrong. I don't want to hurt your fragile
human feelings. One of the reasons I selected you for this
mission is because you have been painfully average. I
want you to deliver a message of hope and encouragement
to humankind! People are my greatest creation. I am
weary of watching most of them fail miserably to live
up to their potential. Life is a great gift. Most of you
are spending your lives just trying to mildly entertain
yourselves until you die, as if you are killing time waiting
for the bus to heaven. Very few of you have goals. It is
hard to hit targets if you don't even have them. I am
giving you an amazing gift. You could call it a mission,
a goal, or simply a higher purpose for living."

"Well," I replied, feeling a mixture of hesitation and curiosity, "one should never look a gift horse in the mouth, but what exactly is this mission?"

"Joe, you are going to deliver a message to the world! It will awaken people to the endless abilities and possibilities I have created in them. Humans are far, far more capable than they realize. They have forgotten they are created in my image. Through me all things are possible!"

Without really understanding what was happening, I found myself totally engaged in the exchange. I typed, "Just how am I going to wake people up? Why would anyone listen to me?"

"Because you are going to prove that the seemingly impossible is possible!"

I thought God already had that department pretty well covered.

"What do you have in mind? Am I going to start flapping my arms and flying? Walk through fire? Speak in tongues?"

"You are going to play in the Masters golf tournament next spring, and if your faith is strong enough, you are going to win. If your faith lags, you may not win, but it'll be fun and helpful for humanity just the same. Don't you think so?"

"You have got to be kidding! Flying would be easier! I am sixty-three years old and hardly play golf anymore. When I do play, I play like the people I used to feel sorry for."

"I don't do a lot of kidding, although I enjoy it occasionally, like the time I let the whole world believe it was going to be a complete disaster when clocks turned 12:01 on January 1, 2000. That was kind of fun."

"That was a joke? You really had us fooled. People thought the world was going to end."

"People need to have more faith."

"You're not joking now? I know I am just a human, and a rather average one at that, so I shouldn't be challenging your thinking process. But why me? Why the Masters?"

"No joke. Again, I chose you because you are so average. It would hardly create the attention I want if some great golfer won the Masters and then gave testimony about how, with faith and belief, a man can do anything. I chose a sports venue because sports have become so important in human society. Sports have become almost a religion. People practically worship great players and favorite teams. Sundays have become more about sports than about church. More people are inclined to listen to a sports hero than to a preacher. I can't blame them. Those television evangelists with the crazy hairdos are becoming harder and harder to take. That's another reason I chose you. You have lousy hair, what there is of it. If you ever try one of those silly comb-overs, I'll be sorely tempted to strike you with lightning. I chose the Masters because golf is an individual sport. This would not make sense in a team situation. Golf takes only average physical ability. It is important this be accomplished by someone considered to be past his prime. One of the lessons I am going to teach through you is that age is a self-imposed limitation. Nobody is too old to achieve great goals.

"This is not going to be nearly as difficult as you suspect. All you have to do is believe absolutely and commit wholeheartedly. Herb and I will take care of the rest."

"Herb?"

"You are going to meet Herb Friday after work. I want you to have a few days to mull this over. Don't judge the book by the cover. He's not much to look at. You and Herb are going to get along wonderfully. He is an interesting guy, part Shivas Irons from Golf in the Kingdom, part Clarence from It's a Wonderful Life, with a little bit of Johnny from Seven Days in Utopia and Curly from City Slickers thrown in. I will e-mail instructions on how to find Herb in a few minutes."

"E-mail? Have you run out of stone tablets?"

"Good one! I'm glad to observe you are already becoming more comfortable conversing with me. A sense of humor almost always makes things easier. It will be a very valuable tool for you during the mission. Most people don't think of me as being humorous. Who do they think invented laughter? If you humans would learn to laugh more, the world would be much better off. People need to stop being so easily offended. You should spend more time laughing with and at each other, instead of pointing fingers all the time.

"One last thing for today: don't tell anyone about this, except Sheila. You will need her support. Other people would likely undermine your faith with their doubts. Other people might even call for the men in the white suits. I will be checking in with you from time to time, to provide inspiration or a spiritual kick in the rear end, if necessary. Keep your sense of humor. Enjoy this ride! And have fun with it!"

CHAPTER 2

||||||||||||||||||||||||||||||||||||||||||||||||||||||||||||||||||||||||||||||||||||||||||||||||||||||||||||||||||||||||||||||||||||||||||||||||||||||||||||||||||||||||||||||||||||||||||||

I LEFT THE BANK. TELLING MY STAFF I NEEDED TO DO SOME FARM inspections. The rest of the morning and the afternoon, I spent driving around the back roads of the county, trying to get my head around what was happening. I had always thought of myself as a good churchgoing believer. I was, for the first time in my life, getting a glimpse of the difference between my routine lukewarm belief and real faith. This was going to be a heck of a test. The first challenge would be telling Sheila. She had always been a very active church member, but she would be getting this story secondhand from me. I thought about it for a while and decided to go with the direct approach. I would tell her what had happened and see whether she called for the guys with the butterfly nets.

I headed for home as the sun was setting, wondering whether our marriage would ever be the same—or whether it might even be over after I told her I'd received chat messages and e-mails from God. For my own part, I truly believed that He'd been in touch with me. Yes, doubt nudged into my mind. I'd questioned my sanity as I drove around checking out the farms, but a deep feeling of peace tinged with wonder pushed the doubt away. I somehow just knew that a great adventure had begun, and I wanted to be involved. I still wondered what Sheila would say as I drove up to the house, hit the garage door opener, and parked inside.

As I walked through the door from our garage, Sheila greeted me with a smile and our customary kiss.

"Hi, honey," I sputtered. "Can you hold dinner for a while? I need to get your take on something that happened to me today. I'll open a bottle of wine and meet you on the back porch."

She gave me a funny look. I knew why too. I didn't usually ask for a powwow over wine right after work. "You didn't get fired, did you?" she asked, the worry obvious in her tone of voice.

I took her by the shoulders and gave her a gentle hug. "No," I said, "I didn't get fired. It's not like that at all. But we have to talk, okay?"

"Sure," she replied, still looking a little apprehensive. She knew me better than anyone else in the world. I knew she could sense I was nervous, and I definitely was. How many guys come home and tell their wives that God sends e-mails just for them? Not too many, I guessed.

"I suppose a little wine, fresh air, and conversation is the perfect way to start an evening," she said, "as long as nothing's wrong. If there is something wrong, I want you to tell me right now. Forget the wine."

"Nothing's wrong, Sheila. Trust me!"

She crossed her arms over her chest. I could tell that she didn't really believe me, that she was giving me the benefit of the doubt. "Okay then," she said, "grab that bottle of Riesling in the fridge; it'll go nicely with our chicken casserole."

We got the wine and went out to the porch. I opened the wine in silence, poured, and waited until she'd had a few sips before I started my story. To her credit, she listened without interrupting, bursting into laughter, or running inside to call Mort, a good friend who also ran a psychiatric practice in town.

"You know, Joe," she said when I was done, obviously suppressing a giggle, "I've always enjoyed the fact that you were a little nuts. It is part of your charm and makes living with you interesting. Now I am wondering if all these years, I have only been seeing the tip of the iceberg. You might be even nuttier than I thought."

Suddenly, a white dove swooped onto the porch and landed on my head. It sat there cooing.

Sheila laughed loudly. "Uh, Joe, you know there's a bird on your head."

"I sort of do!" I said. The dove sat down. I could feel the warmth of its body on my clean pate. I hoped my fine feathery friend didn't need to go to the bathroom.

"Well," Sheila said, still laughing, "what's it doing sitting on your head?"

"Like I said, I saw the dove earlier."

Sheila suddenly stopped laughing. She put her wine glass down. "Uh, Joe, the bird just winked at me. I swear, it just winked at me!"

I had known the dove would do something like that. "It seems to like winking at people," I said.

The dove flew off.

Sheila stared at me in openmouthed amazement. "Oh my God! Did that *really* just happen? Is your condition contagious? Are we both nuts?"

We sat there in stunned silence, not stirring until the smell of burned chicken casserole brought us to our senses. We decided we needed more wine instead of chicken, anyway. I poured another glass. Sheila went into the kitchen and returned with the barely edible unburned portions of the casserole on two plates.

"Okay," Sheila said in between bites. "Since we both saw the dove, we can assume it wasn't just our imaginations. Tell you what ... if this Herb guy checks out for real, I think we should buy into this whole mission thing and see where it takes us."

I set my fork down and dabbed my mouth with a paper napkin. "I agree. I guess we will know Friday afternoon. Remember, I was told that we should not mention this to anyone." I leaned forward and took Sheila's hands in mine. "Do you really believe?" I asked.

She looked serious. Tears formed in her eyes. She nodded and squeezed my hands. "Yes, honey, I believe. I believe not because of signs, like winking doves. I can just sense something is going on. Something more important than we are."

I released her hands and sighed. "I know. I do too. I'm a little scared, though."

"So am I," Sheila said, "but I think that's par for the course."

I laughed. "Par for the course. Good one, Sheila!"

The rest of the week passed in a blur. Spring was always busy at the bank, and this particular April was certainly no exception. Finally, Friday arrived, and my rendezvous with the mysterious Herb drew near. The afternoon dragged on, and the later it got, the more impossible it became to focus on my routine job functions. I kept looking back and forth from my printer to my monitor, wondering whether my imagination had been playing tricks on me after all. It was strange how just a few days of separation could begin to dilute the experience. God had sent no more messages. Five o'clock finally came, and I hurried to my car, anxious to see whether Herb really existed.

Following the directions from God's e-mail, which had arrived in my inbox just minutes after our chat on Monday, I turned down a small dirt road about five miles south of town. I had thought I was familiar with every road in the area, but I realized I had never taken this one. *Talk about "the road less traveled,"* I thought. This one looked as if it hadn't been used in years. It reminded me of the country trails my high school buddies and I had used to sneak around to park with our girlfriends or drink beer. After a mile or so, the road ended at a small clearing. Scattered around the clearing were several small sheds, a garage, a large barn, and an old mobile home with a rickety porch. What really caught my eye was a scruffy driving range, along with a well-bunkered putting green.

I braked to a stop and turned off the ignition, waiting for the dust cloud I had created to swirl past me before I got out of the car. Wow! If this was the start of the trail that would lead me to the Masters, I was certainly a long way from the finish. Hearing a friendly yapping noise, I looked down and saw an old dachshund coming toward me. She was

14

moving about as quickly as her age and short legs would allow. The dog assumed the upright prairie dog sitting posture in front of me, unique to dachshunds. This trait makes them irresistible but impossible to take seriously.

I've owned several dachshunds. Not the most trainable breed. Dachshunds won't herd cattle or pull a sleigh through the snow, and they haven't a clue about what to do if Timmy falls into the well. Maybe their purpose is to provide an example of pure, simple affection, or at least additional living proof of God's sense of humor.

Reaching down to give the old girl a pat, I noticed a small sign around her neck. In crude, barely legible letters, it read, "Joe, go to the practice tee. Hit some warm-up shots. I'll be there in a little while. Dog's name is Tootie. She's smarter than she looks. God told me the same thing about you. Herb."

"Okay, Tootie," I said, giving her ears a rub, "let's do as Herb says. But I hope he realizes at my age, by the time I get warmed up, I'm tired."

I took my clubs out of the trunk, put on my golf shoes, and followed Tootie to the practice tee. The practice tee was different from any I had ever seen. It was about fifty yards long. Only a five- or six-yard strip was closely mown and flat. The remainder included varying degrees of slopes and grass heights, along with a fairway bunker. Standing on the tee, I noticed another unusual feature. Unlike other practice tees, which were always located on one end or the other of the range, this tee was situated at what appeared to be the middle of the range. A large bucket of shiny new tour-quality balls sat on the mowed strip. I stretched a little, made a dozen or so practice swings, and started hitting half-lob shots with my sand wedge. After a few leisurely swings, I eased into a nice rhythm and gradually worked my way through my longer clubs.

Hitting range balls by myself has always had an hypnotic, mesmerizing effect. The feeling of my various body parts working together in near-perfect harmony when I am swinging well is one of the things I enjoy most about golf. No worrying about a score or what anybody else scrutinizing my swing might think. Just total immersion, completely peaceful and effortless. Why this sensation never seemed to transfer seamlessly to the golf course had always been a mystery to me. If I had been able to take the same effortless rhythm and confidence from the range to the golf course, I would have been one heck of a player.

On my second five-iron shot, a voice interrupted me. "Not bad for a stove-up old banker." I half-topped the shot and turned for my first look at Herb. He was about twenty yards away, approaching with Tootie. As forewarned, Herb wasn't an impressive physical specimen. Tall and slightly stooped, he had the look of either a sixty-five-year-old who had lived a hard life or a ninety-year-old who had taken good care of himself. Whichever the case, in the round of life, Herb had already "made the turn" and was somewhere out on the back nine. Gray hair protruded from beneath an ancient brown corduroy snap-billed golf cap. His skin had the ruddy look of someone who had spent way too much time in the sun without the benefit of sunscreen lotions. He wore a faded pair of jeans with a golf shirt that had been red at one time but was now well on its way to pink. If central casting had been called on to provide a character actor to play the part of a hillbilly golf pro, they would have sent someone who looked a lot like Herb. His emerald-green eyes were his most startling feature. Piercing and intelligent, they were windows to a kind and peaceful soul. I had never considered reincarnation, but his eyes reflected wisdom unattainable in a single lifetime.

Shaking my hand, he grinned and introduced himself. "Herb. But I guess the Big Guy has already told you about me."

"Glad to meet you," I replied. "I am relieved to see that you actually exist. I have to admit that I have been a bit slow about believing this is all happening. Seems like it could still be all in my imagination, but you sure seem to be real enough. You know, self-doubt and all that stuff."

"Would it help if I pinched you to show you I'm real? I assure you that I am quite real." Herb kicked the turf with the tip of his golf shoe. "Can't say as I blame you for having your doubts, though," he said.

"What you just said leads me to explain how this is going to work. My part of this mission is to hone your skills. Your part of the mission is to turn your doubt into faith. It will take both skill and faith to be successful."

I picked up a golf ball and rolled it around in my right hand, feeling the dimples, the weight. The ball in my hand somehow comforted me, made me feel more at ease with Herb. "I'm not sure I'm up to the task," I said, bowing my head.

"I'd worry about you if you thought you'd have no obstacles to overcome. Look, I've been watching you with my binoculars out the window of the house. Wanted to see what your swing looked like when you weren't trying to impress anybody. Few golfers swing the same when someone is watching them as they do when they're alone. Liked what I saw. Easy to tell you used to be a pretty good player. We won't need to change your basic action much at all. Hit a few more for me, will ya?"

I said sure, raked a couple of balls from the stack, and hit them, extremely conscious of Herb's presence. Predictably, neither of these swings was anywhere as smooth as my earlier efforts. Herb nodded sagely. It was obvious that he wasn't at all surprised by what he was seeing. After several more unsatisfying shots, he asked me to stop and suggested we sit down on an old bench at the edge of the tee.

We walked over to the bench and sat down together. Herb stretched his arms straight out in front of him. "Pretty darned obvious where we need to start, isn't it?" he queried, eyes sparkling with delight. "You've got a very functional golf swing. We just need to get your brain out of the way."

"I'm all for that," I responded. "I've always heard the way winners win is by playing to their strengths. I don't know any bankers who could honestly say their brain was their strength."

Herb chuckled. "It's not just bankers. Everybody struggles with the brain problem, even the touring pros. A golf swing can be and should be about as natural as walking or chewing your food, especially for a player who has been playing and practicing for years. Problem is, all golfers, pro and amateur alike, get thrown off by outside stimuli, especially the stimulus they have labeled 'pressure.' Throw in enough pressure, and anybody's game will unravel."

I coughed and looked away, knowing he was right.

"You okay?" he asked.

I nodded and then pivoted to face him. "So pressure is the enemy?"

"Pressure is absolutely the enemy, and like many negative things in life, it's only a figment of your own imagination. Despite how much television announcers love to talk vividly about players succumbing to pressure, there is no such thing as pressure. It doesn't exist. It is merely an illusion. A few minutes ago, you created the illusion of pressure when you became aware that I was watching you swing. Before I was a part of your swinging environment, you were swinging at a level very close to the best of your ability. I arrived, introducing only a slight change in the environment, and your swing changed dramatically, in response to what you would describe as pressure created by the experience of having your swing critiqued."

I stood up.

"Where you going?" Herb asked.

"I can't sit still. Too much pressure."

Herb laughed. "Look at it this way," he said as he stood up too. "God did a pretty darn good job designing this old world of ours. He created only good things. Almost everything exists at some point along a scale from 0 to 100 percent. For instance, there is no such thing as 'cold,' only the absence of heat in varying degrees. At zero degrees, there is no heat. You can continue along up the scale to moderately hot, all the way to hot as hell."

Herb clapped me on the back, almost knocking the wind out of me. The man didn't know his own strength. "Easy, Herb!"

We began walking back to the tee. Herb continued talking, and I listened intently as he explained that there was no such thing as dark, only the absence of light. He said there was no such thing as ignorance, only the lack of knowledge. There was no such thing as prejudice, only the lack of acceptance.

"You see where I'm heading here?" Herb asked. He stopped walking and faced me with his hands on his hips.

"I think so," I said.

"There is no such thing as pressure, only the lack of focus and confidence. The less focused and confident a golfer feels, the more he thinks he is feeling pressure, when in reality he is only feeling less focused and less confident."

I nodded sagely, pretending to understand; I didn't want to look as stupid as I felt. Herb had certainly caught me off guard. There was obviously a lot more to this guy than I had gathered from my first impression. I half-expected him to start levitating.

"Try hitting a few more shots, without worrying about swing mechanics or what I might be thinking about your swing. Just focus on being confident and smooth."

Scraping a few balls out of the pile with my five-iron, I began hitting shots down the range. They weren't much better than those Herb had already seen.

"Hold up a second," Herb grunted. "You didn't quite catch on to what I was explaining. You've merely shifted from thinking about me watching you to thinking about not thinking. It is impossible for the human brain to 'not' anything. If I told you not to think about an elephant, your mind would immediately conjure up the image of an elephant. Since you have to focus on something, focus on being relaxed and confident. This is the secret to being able to take your practice swing to the course."

At this point, it crossed my mind to wonder which one of us was crazier, Herb with his theories or me for listening to them. Although it was awkward at first, my focus gradually improved, and I started to hit shots similar to those I'd been making before Herb appeared.

Herb nodded in approval and asked me to sit down on the bench with him again. I wasn't sure I wanted more philosophy. I was tired. It had been a long week, and what with God e-mailing me, it had also been pretty strange. But I sat down again. Tootie sat on my toes and licked my hand, obviously soliciting an ear massage.

"Even at your present level of ability," he continued, "you would be better than scratch if you could somehow produce the best effort you are capable of for each shot. Consider this: If you put an eighteen-handicapper and a touring pro side by side, hitting shots all day at a hole one hundred yards away, at the end of the day, there would not be any appreciable difference between the pro's best shot and the eighteen-handicapper's best shot. Both would either have a hole in one or a leaner. However, there would be a significant difference between the pro's average shot and the average shot from the eighteen-handicapper. The biggest difference would be between the eighteen-handicapper's worst shot and the pro's worst shot. The eighteen-handicapper would likely skull a few shots thirty yards over the green and completely chunk others. The pro would never miss a shot so badly."

I told Herb I got it. I said so again when he went on to say that the major difference between a great player and an average player is that the great player performs closer to his maximum ability on almost every shot. The great player accomplishes this consistent performance by adhering to a strict routine and focusing on a small, specific target. If the average player could somehow summon up his best effort every time, the only difference between him and the pro would be the pro's ability to hit the ball farther.

"Speaking of distance," I interjected, "isn't that going to be a huge problem? Championship golf courses have become brutally long, particularly Augusta National, where they have recently made it considerably longer. Even with the hotter new balls and better clubs, I am going to have a hard time reaching greens in regulation."

Herb nodded in agreement. "Challenging but not impossible. I am going to teach you a variety of strengthening and flexibility exercises. These exercises, coupled with some tweaking of your technique, will increase your distance at least 10 percent. We'll tack on a little more distance with some special equipment I've designed for you. Although you will no doubt be the shortest hitter in the tournament, we will make up for your lack of distance by increasing your accuracy with longer-range approach shots and by developing an almost perfect short game."

Herb, Tootie, and I left the bench and wandered down the range, retrieving the balls I had hit. Tootie enthusiastically ran along gathering balls and bringing them to us, being rewarded with pats on the head for each retrieved ball. Herb certainly liked to talk. I supposed it was awfully lonely way out here with just his dog. He continued to expound upon his theories for dealing with pressure by increasing one's ability to ignore the situation and focus on one's inner self. I guessed, given the quirky circumstances, he was just about what I should have expected as my God-assigned guru. Or maybe he was some sort of personification of God?

"Isn't this going to take a lot of time? Wouldn't it be a whole lot simpler if God just gave me more strength and flexibility? It worked for Samson, and as bad as my hair is, I promise not to let anybody cut it ... Or for that matter, God could just cause my ball to bounce off sprinkler heads, hop along cart paths, glance off trees, or whatever it takes to help me score like a pro."

Herb shook his head and then fixed those incredible eyes on mine. "Listen closely. You need to get this. This isn't about God winning the Masters. Everyone who believes in God believes God is capable of doing anything. Compared to creating the universe, parting the Red Sea, or raising His Son from the dead, winning a golf tournament is rather miniscule, don't you think?"

Herb stooped over to pick up another ball. As he stood back up, he said, "Our mission, our message to deliver, is to wake people to the realization God has given human beings much, much more ability than they have been using. There truly is greatness within each of us. You are going to demonstrate to the world how an average man, with average abilities, can achieve greatness with enough faith and belief. Hopefully, this will inspire others to stop imposing limits on themselves, get off their rear ends, and fulfill their potential. As the old saying goes, imagine what you could accomplish if you were convinced nothing was impossible."

"Sorry. Didn't want to imply I wasn't all on board and ready to do my part. I am just concerned about finding the time. My life is already pretty hectic."

We began walking back toward the house and my car. I was happy about that. As much as I was enjoying Herb's ramblings, I wanted to go home.

"You already have enough time. You just aren't using it wisely. You need to change your concept of what a day is. Like most folks, your concept of a day is the number of hours from six o'clock in the morning when your alarm goes off until about eleven in the evening, when you finally turn off the television and go to bed. We are going to change your concept of what a day is. You are going to start going to bed at nine and getting up at four."

"Whoa!" I protested. "What if I told you I'm just not a morning person?"

Herb shrugged and replied, "People say they aren't 'morning people.' They are wrong. God designed us to be morning people. That's why dawn is the freshest, most uplifting part of the day. Folks have defeated the design by staying up too late. It is very hard to be a morning person if you stagger to bed after eleven. You are simply going to start trading two highly unproductive hours you spend from nine o'clock until eleven in the evening for two highly productive hours from four in the morning until six. That's a bargain! You will be amazed at how your life will change. Teach this trick to your kids. I guarantee it will make them successful. It is hard to lose if you have a two-hour head start on the rest of the world every day.

"As the president of that little bank, you have some flexibility. Tell your staff that until further notice, you are going to start coming in around seven in the morning and leaving at around three in the afternoon."

This made sense. I could get more done early in the morning, without the constant interruptions from customers and staff. My doctor had been after me to lose a little weight. I would tell everyone I was using this different schedule to work on my golf game as a form of exercise.

We stopped in front of my car. Herb picked Tootie up and cradled her in his arms. "I get that this is all a bit much for you to take in right now. I understand. God understands."

I told him it was kind of intimidating, but I was willing to hang in there. Gesturing toward the practice tee, I commented, "I've never seen a practice tee like this one. The small section where I was hitting balls is the only part that resembles a normal practice tee."

"I built this tee so you could practice golf, not just swing mechanics. Very little actual golf is played from perfectly flat lies, yet almost all practice ranges are flat. This range has about every combination of slope and grass height imaginable, so you can practice hitting shots from lies you typically encounter on the course, including fairway bunkers. Did you notice the trees down at the other end?"

I nodded yes.

"They are for practicing restricted swing shots and learning to control trajectory. I put the tee in the middle of the range so that you can hit balls in any direction. This allows you to practice hitting shots into the wind, downwind, and with every type of crosswind."

Herb pulled an old pocket watch out of his front pocket. The fob at the end of the short brass chain looked like some old medallion. Glancing at the watch, Herb said, "That's enough for today. Tootie gets grumpy if she doesn't get supper on time. Let's meet here tomorrow at about three thirty. I think I'll be done with some of the new equipment I mentioned before. We can try it out, and then I'd like to go over the basic plan with you."

"Plan? I thought the plan was just to win the Masters."

"That's part of the problem with most folks—they can articulate some great goal they have, but it never gets any farther than just being a glorified dream because they don't have a detailed plan about how to achieve it. People need to realize that accomplishing a great goal requires the accomplishment of a series of small bite-size goals. They are steps to the ultimate goal. If you try to eat an elephant all in one bite, it never happens. See you tomorrow." He shook my hand firmly and then turned toward the old mobile home.

I watched Herb enter the house, and then I got in the car and drove off.

"What have I gotten myself into?" I whispered.

CHAPTER 3

||||||||||||||||||||||||||||||||||||||||||||||||||||||||||||||||||||||||||||||||||||||||||||||||||||||||||||||||||||||||||||||||||||||||||||||||||||||||||||

TUESDAY MORNING WAS UNEVENTFUL. OVER BREAKFAST, I TOLD Sheila about my plans to change my schedule. She was all for it. She had been after me for months to exercise more. I had been burning myself out at the office. She gave me a kiss, swatted me on the rear, and pointed at the door. "I don't know how this whole mission thing is going to work out," she said with a smile, "but in a worst-case scenario, at least maybe you will lose a little bit of weight."

Losing weight sounded like a good idea, I told her. I headed to work with a feeling of accomplishment, a notion that my life was changing for the better already, and I'd only just begun my journey with Herb. At my desk, I booted up my computer, not knowing what to expect. To my relief it was a normal launch into cyberspace. No shaking monitors or gold-colored printouts. I quickly sent an e-mail to the staff, advising them of my new work schedule.

Our compliance officer, Nick Crawford, popped into my office a little after nine. "Hey, boss," he chirped. "Nice job on those two reports yesterday. I looked them over, and this is the first time you didn't make any mistakes. Did someone help you with them?"

If he only knew. "Well, Nick," I replied, "even a clock that's stopped is right twice a day. I am bound to get them right once in a while."

Nick was a nice young guy. He used to caddy for me when he was a kid. I had jumped at the chance to hire him five years ago when he graduated from a small liberal arts college. His art history degree wasn't much of a fit for banking, but his personality definitely was. I knew upon hiring him that the older ladies working at the bank would take to him like he was a grandson. I was right. They absolutely loved him and went out of their way to show him the ropes.

Nick was also bright. He instinctively understood that a great way to obtain job security is to discover the part of your boss's job that he or she hates and learn to do it, relieving your boss of the task. You then become the last person the boss would think about letting go if the company downsized. This insight led Nick to volunteer to become our compliance officer. Regulatory compliance has become the bane of community banking. A good portion of it is pure nonsense. Small banks have proven to be very resilient when it comes to surviving adverse business cycles, natural disasters, inflation, deflation, and so on. However, they are no match for the federal government. It isn't a fair fight. The feds continue to devise new regulations and then implement them with vague guidelines, fining community banks or threatening to close them if they don't comply with the letter of the law.

Trouble is, you can call one of their so-called experts for instructions about how to comply with a new regulation and later be in really hot water with an examiner who totally disagrees with the expert's interpretation about how you should have complied. Community banks are being regulated out of business. It is a shame. Small banks provide most of the funding for small businesses, and small businesses provide most of the jobs in America. The regulators are driving the nails into the coffin in which the American dream is being buried. As the president of a small bank myself, I found myself more and more at odds with regulations that threatened to undo all the good we did.

"We should be in decent shape to handle the exit interview with the examiners Friday," Nick continued. "You set that up for two o'clock, right?"

"That's correct. Looking forward to it like a root canal. Let's meet with the audit committee to go over our responses right after lunch Friday."

Nick gave me a thumbs-up and headed back to his office. Leaving the bank later in the afternoon, I felt a growing sense of purpose. Life had become very routine, sort of like those lines from that Eagles song, "Desperado": "You're losin' all your highs and lows. Ain't it funny how the feeling goes away?" I had become comfortable and content, maybe a little too comfortable. I had a lot of groundhog days like in that old movie starring Bill Murray. Here I was, entering the last third of my life, without having accomplished anything memorable. If I ever had great-great-grandchildren, would they know who I was? What I had done? Scary to think about how soon I would be forgotten. I'd heard it said that our one shot at immortality was to be remembered. I had certainly blown my shot, but perhaps now I might have another chance.

My banking career had become increasingly less interesting, as the government regulations seemed hell-bent on dumbing down banking. Rules had been written to make banking very generic, with little room for creativity. I supposed this was to enable young bank examiners to better understand the business, but it was akin to letting the newly minted second lieutenants run the army, ignoring the wisdom of more experienced officers. This adventure was just what I needed. It had been a long time since I had been so engaged and excited. I could hardly wait to see what today's session would bring. I drove slowly down the lane to Herb's place, trying to stir up as little dust as possible. Herb and his sawed-off canine sidekick greeted me as I pulled into the clearing.

"Don't bother getting all your clubs out today, Joe, just a wedge to warm up with," he said. "I've got the new clubs for you to try. We won't hit many shots today. You are probably a little sore from yesterday. After a few shots, we'll head on over to the porch to strategize. Warm up with your wedge. We'll try the new clubs once you're good and loose."

I grabbed my lob wedge and followed Herb to the range. Tootie reluctantly tagged along beside us, every small step taking her farther from her beloved dinner bowl. I did a few stretches. Herb was right.

After a winter of inactivity, my old muscles were stiff from yesterday's exertion.

I hit several easy wedge shots. Once Herb could tell I had settled into a decent rhythm, he asked me to stop. Grinning like a new father showing off his baby son, he took two clubs out of a long sack. I had never seen anything quite like these clubs. They were both about four inches longer than my driver. They appeared to have heads similar to a five-wood. Both had extra-long grips. The grips had colored bands on them at staggered intervals. The face on one of them was significantly closed, and the face of the other was open to a similar degree.

Responding to my curious look, Herb offered an explanation. "These clubs are part of your compensation for lack of distance. Given your moderate length off the tee, you are going to be faced with much longer approach shots than the golfers you will be competing against. The graphite shafts on these clubs are more flexible than those on your present clubs. They will add some distance but require swing adjustments on your part. I estimate you will be able to hit them about 230 yards when you grip at the end, ranging down to about 200 yards if you choke to the bottom band on the grip."

Herb handed me the closed-face club, and I raked over a ball from the stack. My first two shots were ugly smothered hooks. Herb suggested I try a slightly more upright swing and start at the full-choke grip position, gradually working my way to the end of the grip as I became more comfortable with the feel of the club. "Slow down at the top," he admonished. "These softer shafts require a much smoother transition than your stiffer clubs. One of Jack Nicklaus's favorite swing thoughts was to make sure he completed his backswing before starting the downswing. Give that a try. Worked pretty well for Jack."

In a matter of minutes, I was amazed at the shots the club was producing—high, gentle ball flights, somewhere between a draw and a hook. I tried the open-faced club and soon got comfortable with it, producing high shots with curvatures slightly more than a fade, but not what you would call a real slice. In spite of my soreness, this was fun!

"Okay, Joe, let's stop here," Herb suggested. "Don't want to overdo it. Looks like these clubs are going to work fine. I love the ball flight. The trajectory and spin you are producing are just what we need. It will take some time to fine-tune the distances from each grip position, but we are well on our way. Let's head for the porch for a cold one, and I'll give you a rough outline of how we are going to pull this off."

I was excited about these new clubs. They were great! I was reluctant to stop the practice session; I had never had more pure fun just hitting balls. But Herb was right. I was a little sore from yesterday's activity. I was also more than a little curious about the upcoming strategy session. I cleaned the clubs with a towel, stuffed them in my bag, and joined Herb as he ambled over to his house. Tootie impatiently led the way, no doubt sensing dinner was at hand.

"What do you think we should call these contraptions?" Herb asked as we walked along. "As your caddy, I would get tired of your asking for the extra-long, slightly closed-faced five-wood or the extra-long, slightly open-faced five-wood. We might get penalized for slow play if we went through that routine every time."

Looking at the two clubs protruding above the rest of the clubs in my bag, I had a bit of inspiration. "Let's call them 'Hotch,'" I answered. "Hook Hotch and Slice Hotch."

"Works for me," Herb replied. "How did you come up with that?"

"Sudden inspiration. I grew up in a family of very average-height people. None of the males in our family are over five-ten, with the exception of my older brother, Bill Ed. He is six-three. My dad started calling Bill Ed 'Hot Shot' after he hit a home run in a Little League game, and it stuck, gradually morphing into just 'Hotch.' Our family photos look a little odd, with Hotch towering over the rest of us. Strangers who see the pictures often ask if he was adopted, or perhaps a foreign exchange student who lived with us for a while. He was the best golfer in the family, largely because he was the only one of us who could putt worth a hoot. Bill Ed is gradually working his way back from a severe stroke he suffered a few months ago. I think he would get a kick out of having these clubs as namesakes."

"That's cool," Herb responded. "Just one more thing to feel good about. A mission like this always spawns some beneficial sidebars."

We arrived at the porch and sat down in two old rocking chairs flanking a large metal dog bowl. "You've been on other missions like this? How many times?" I asked as I looked out over the practice range.

"More than I care to count," he answered, grinning. Herb got up, stepped just inside the screen door, and rummaged through a cupboard visible from the porch. He returned with a can of dog food and a spoon. "In current vernacular, let's just say this definitely isn't my first rodeo."

Tootie stood anxiously by as Herb spooned food into her bowl. She practically dove into the bowl. Completely engrossed in her feeding frenzy, she appeared oblivious to Herb's friendly pat on her rear end.

Herb excused himself once more and disappeared inside, returning shortly with two glasses of what appeared to be iced tea. The look on my face must have told Herb that my idea of "having a cold one" was beer-related. "You're officially in training now," he stated as he handed me a glass and sat in the rocking chair next to me. "We are going to limit your consumption of alcohol. The stuff kills brain cells, and you don't have many extra ones. This is my special herbal tea. Shouldn't be too surprising, coming from a guy named Herb. Supposed to relax and energize you simultaneously." We clinked our glasses together and took large gulps. The concoction wasn't too bad. I guessed I could get used to a new nonbeer thirst quencher.

Herb became serious. "Let's talk about our plan. Your confidence and commitment will be fueled by your belief in our plan. The first part of any good plan is an accurate assessment of where you are now—the starting point, so to speak. So what's your assessment of your golf game?"

"Well," I replied, taking a refreshing sip of the tea, "I guess it would be helpful to begin by telling you how my game arrived at its present state."

Herb nodded agreement.

"Okay," I continued. "My dad and I were very close. He was my hero—a hard worker with a strong faith and an even stronger sense of values. He was the best golfer in town. I naturally wanted to be like him. I started tagging along with him at the golf course. When I was big enough, I caddied for him. He gradually allowed me to hit a few shots during a round. Once I showed a real interest, he began teaching me the game. It didn't take long for a strong passion to develop. I liked baseball and basketball, but golf was my thing. I practiced constantly and often played thirty-six holes a day in the summer. By the time I graduated from high school, I was good enough to be offered a full-ride college scholarship."

Herb smiled at me. I somehow got the feeling he already knew my story. Looking back on it, I think he did and was just humoring me. I told him that I realized I'd never make it big in golf while I was in college. I knew I was a small frog in a big pond. So I decided to concentrate on work and school. I explained that I'd continued to play golf after graduation and that I'd even won several local amateur events. I was probably the best player in the area for about a ten-year span.

"I knew you had some talent, Joe," Herb said. He laughed and gave Tootie a pat on the head. Then he continued my story for me. "But life got in the way of your passions, didn't it?"

I nodded.

"Happens to most of us, I'm afraid," he said.

"My game suffered as I got caught up in work. To be honest, I was embarrassed. I was known as this really good golfer, so it was humiliating to struggle to break eighty. Now, about the only golf I play is four-person scrambles in charity fundraisers. I haven't turned in enough individual scores over the past three years to maintain an official handicap. If I played a round under strict tournament rules, I bet I would probably shoot around eighty-five. I guess that's our starting point."

"That's about what I was anticipating," Herb replied. "Your story is not uncommon. Many players get into the vicious cycle of poor scores creating less enjoyment, which makes them play less, so they score even worse and want to play even less. It's a shame so many people attach their enjoyment to the score. Many golfers would experience greater enjoyment from the game if they didn't try to play the same game as the pros on television, where the eighteen-hole score is what it's all about. They would have more fun if they approached the game the way a bunch of kids would. Just enjoy each hole. Create a different game for each hole. Play one hole where you have to hit at least two shots left-handed, another hole requiring each player to be in at least one bunker or hit every shot with a five-iron. There are endless variations to just have fun with the game. It doesn't have to be so darn serious all the time. Whoops! Got off the subject there for a while. Need to get back on task."

"You do get on sometimes, Herb! I barely know you, but I can see you like to talk."

We both remained silent for a long moment. It was as if Herb was gathering his strength for another go, and he was.

"The good news for us is there is a heck of a lot of difference between an eighty-five-shooter who used to be scratch and an eighty-five-shooter who has never been any better. You have most of the physical and mental skills; they are just a little rusty."

"A little! I'd say I need some sandpaper to get the rust off. Maybe something even harsher," I said. I stretched my legs out in front of me, picked up the glass of tea, and swirled the liquid around in the glass, causing the ice to ring against the sides. "I have to admit, I feel a little overwhelmed."

Several crows landed on the green. They cackled loudly.

"The best way to achieve a big goal is to work backward from the goal itself," Herb said. "In your case, for example, in order to win the Masters Tournament, you first have to qualify for an invitation to play in the tournament. There are several ways to automatically earn an invitation, most of which aren't going to happen for you, such as being in the top fifty in the world rankings or having won a recent major championship. Your only chance at getting an invitation is to win one of the important amateur titles. Your best shot is the Mid-Amateur tournament in September. The Mid-Amateur has an age requirement. Players have to be at least twenty-five years old. This eliminates the college players, as well as most of the guys who are seriously pursuing careers as tournament players. They have usually turned pro by the time they're twenty-five. It is relatively simple to qualify for the Mid-Amateur. You have to prove your amateur status and have an established handicap of 3.7 or less, along with not being a convicted ax-murderer.

"Moving backward, the preceding step for playing in and winning the Mid-Amateur is to have a golf game strong enough to qualify for the tournament. As I said, one of the requirements is to have an established handicap of no higher than 3.7. Based on your self-assessment, you currently play to a ten or eleven handicap. We need to whittle eight strokes off your handicap. Most of this can be done by sharpening your short game. I bet if you looked back at your process of slipping from a scratch player to an eighty-shooter, it was mostly the result of an increasingly clumsy short game. In situations where you used to get down in two shots, you began taking three shots more often than not."

I told Herb he was right. I sighed and shook my head. "I could get depressed."

Herb punched me lightly on the arm and said that as an experienced player I was no doubt aware that the short game entailed pitching, chipping, and putting. He said he was going to give me a pitching system that would vastly improve my effectiveness, with very little alteration of my present technique. I wasn't sure I believed him. I wasn't sure I could do what he asked.

"I'll also teach you an improved technique for chipping and putting. They are basically the same stroke, except with different clubs. We will also work on your thought processes. Remember I told you how your perception of pressure and lack of focus have a negative impact on your game? As your caddy, I will do almost all the thinking for you, until you gradually become capable of running your brain by yourself. At this point, all you need to do is have complete trust in me. Our rough timetable is to establish your handicap at 3.7 or lower in time to register for the Mid-Amateur Tournament, which is played in September."

I stood up and began pacing, careful not to trip on some of the loose boards on the porch. "That's a tall order, Herb."

"You've got friends in high places."

"Yeah," I said, turning to Herb, "but He said there's no guarantee any of this is going to work."

"He always says that. He just wants to keep you on your toes," Herb said.

Herb patted my empty chair. "Sit down, Joe! Your pacing is making me jittery. Tootie's going to get a sore neck watching you walk back and forth like that."

I complied. "Okay, go on."

Herb explained that between the time I was officially registered and the arrival of September, we'd further develop my game to the point where I could win the tournament. After winning the Mid-Am, we'd have the rest of the fall, all winter, and early spring to prepare for the Masters.

"A good portion of the weather between now and next April will be too cold to play or practice in," I said.

I should have known Herb would have an answer.

"We will do some of our best work during the cold months," Herb countered. "Most of your improvement will come from sharpening your short game and improving your focus, both of which can be done inside."

"It sounds so matter-of-fact and simple when you lay it out like that," I sputtered. "But it's sort of like telling me that to fly to England, all I have to do is learn to flap my arms really fast, gradually build up from flying one mile to two miles and so on, until I can fly across the Atlantic by a scheduled date."

"Not the best analogy I have ever heard," Herb replied. "People aren't equipped to fly, but you have all the physical capacity to hit the golf shots it takes to win the Masters, provided you hit the best shot you are capable of almost every time.

"That, my friend, is precisely what you are going to learn to do. Check your Bible. If you have faith the size of a tiny mustard seed, you can move mountains. Hitting a golf ball is considerably easier than moving a mountain. Keep your faith. We are going to accomplish this by completing one well-planned step at a time.

"The rest of this week, we'll keep the practice sessions pretty short. Don't want to hit too many balls until your swing muscles get stretched out a bit. I have arranged a tee time for us this Sunday afternoon at the Hemphill Woods Country Club. Connell Thomas, the head pro, is an old friend. They are having a big member-guest tournament Sunday morning. Almost all his members participate in the tournament. The course should be almost vacant in the afternoon."

I glanced at my watch. "I better head for home, Herb. Don't want to keep Sheila waiting for dinner."

"Good idea, Joe. We accomplished a lot today. I can see we are a good team. This is going to be hard work, but lots of fun."

CHAPTER 4

||||||||||||||||||||||||||||||||||||||||||||||||||||||||||||||||||||||||||||||||||||||||||||||||||||||||||||||||||||||||||||||||||||||||||||||||||||||||||||||||||

ALTHOUGH I'D JUST BEGUN TO GET TO KNOW HERB, MY TIMES WITH him were already becoming a respite from the boredom of my routine life. Things were about to get a little less boring at the bank, though, and the excitement was anything but pleasant. The Friday afternoon closeout session with bank examiners turned out to be as painful as the root canal I'd joked with Nick about.

The bank examiners had been in the bank for ten days the previous month and were back to deliver the results of their findings. Nick Crawford and I, along with two of our board members from the bank's audit committee—Fletcher Leslie, our longtime board chairman, and Dina Cervantes, Wally's only daughter—met in my office to prepare for the closeout session shortly before it was to begin.

Fletcher was legendary in the local farming community. His family had farmed for generations in the valley. He was revered for his farming expertise as well as for his generosity in helping neighbors survive tough times. A consummate good citizen, he had served many terms on local and statewide agricultural boards, and he strongly supported local churches and charities. I had no trouble attracting farm customers. Most of the local farmers wanted to bank with Fletcher. For all his softheartedness, he was a keen, practical businessman. His insight and leadership over the years had been critical to the bank's success.

Dina and I had been friends from grade school. She was the only one of Wally's children who had stayed in town. She had married her high school steady a few weeks after graduation. His family ran a very successful farm supply business. After his father retired, he and Dina had taken took over the business and had done very well. Wally had required her to work at the bank during high school. As such, she had much more than a layman's knowledge of banking.

My assistant, Betti, poked her head in the door. "They just arrived. I told them to set up in the board room and that you would be with them in a couple of minutes."

After a collective sigh, we got up from our chairs and made our way to the boardroom.

The examiner in charge, Marsha Gregory, greeted us cordially, shaking hands with each of us as we entered the room. When everyone was seated at our large oblong conference table, she got down to business.

"Good to see you again," she began. "I'm sure you will remember my colleagues, Charles Swartz and Cynthia Ortega. Please just call me Mars. I am hoping to keep this nonadversarial and productive. We are in the process of finalizing your examination report. We will submit the completed report to the district office after we have added input from this closeout session."

The first hour was devoted to the safety and soundness portions of the examination. As expected, Mars was highly complimentary of the bank. Our loan portfolio was very strong, with almost no problem loans. The examiners agreed with the results of our own internal loan-grading process. In their opinion, we had properly identified any risk in our loan portfolio and had taken proper steps to protect against losses. Documentation in our loan files was satisfactory. On the operations side of the bank, they could find no issues with our depository procedures, dual controls, security systems, and so on.

Then the hammer fell. Mars turned the meeting over to Cynthia Ortega for the compliance portion of the review. Ms. Ortega was an attractive Hispanic lady who appeared to be in her midtwenties. She had never worked in a bank. The FDIC had hired her shortly after she graduated from college. She stood at the head of the table and addressed the group.

"I'm afraid our review of your compliance procedures revealed some serious deficiencies," she said. "The areas of concern involve compliance with the Community Reinvestment Act, truth in lending, fair lending, right of rescission, and flood certifications.

"With regard to the Community Reinvestment Act, as you know, you are required by the act to have a copy of your performance evaluation 'public file' available for public review in your bank. Every employee is supposed to know the location of the public file. During our examination last month, we asked one of your tellers, Aurora Townley, if we could see your public file. Ms. Townley indicated she did not know about the existence of said public file, let alone where it might be located. Do you have an explanation for this deficiency?"

A little amused, I said, "As a matter of fact, I do have an explanation. The day in question was Ms. Townley's second day on the job. We had hired her the day before. During her first day on the job, we thought it was more important to tell her where the fire extinguishers and the restrooms are since we have never had anyone come into the bank and ask to see our public file. However, if you had asked any teller other than Ms. Townley, they would have been able to tell you the location. I've never understood why it is so darn critical for every employee in the bank to know where our public file is kept. On the rare chance that some wild-eyed community activist were to come rushing into the bank demanding to see it, I don't think it is unreasonable to expect this person to wait a few minutes for us to hook him or her up with our officer in charge of CRA. Since it is hard to imagine that one of these community activists actually holds down a real job, it is difficult to understand how they could be so hard-pressed for time."

Fletcher unsuccessfully tried to suppress a chuckle at my response. This did not sit well with Ms. Ortega. "We take CRA compliance very seriously," she stated. "In order for us to resolve this particular violation, we will need a detailed written response addressing your plans to ensure this won't happen again."

After a brief glance at her notes, Ms. Ortega continued. "Our examination of a large sampling of your recent loans revealed problems with your calculations of annual percentage rate disclosures, as required by truth-in-lending regulations. We found errors on two of your loans. The APR on a home equity loan made to Welborn Raymondson was calculated at 7.234 percent. The APR was actually 7.311 percent. The APR on an unsecured personal loan to Irene Vasquez was calculated at 11.421 percent. The APR was actually 11.552 percent. Can you explain how these errors happened?"

"Sure I can. These APR calculations are somewhat complicated and subject to occasional human errors. The underlying issue is that no real harm has been done. Our borrowers know what the base rates on their loans are. The most important information to them is the amount of the monthly payment. They are generally aware that extra costs such as loan fees and recording fees add to the cost of their loan, but they couldn't care less whether it works out that the APR is 7.234 percent or 7.311 percent. Let me ask your two colleagues a question: do either of you have a home mortgage or any other personal loans?"

They both nodded.

"Can either of you tell me what the APR is on any debt you personally have?"

Reddening slightly, they both confessed they couldn't.

"If the APRs on your own loans aren't important enough for you to remember them, what makes you think APRs are important to anyone else? Our occasional miscalculation by about a tenth of a percent certainly isn't enough for the FDIC to get riled up about."

Although I thought my point had been well made, it had about the same effect on the examiners as one might achieve by shooting a duck with a water pistol. I was not impressing Ms. Ortega.

"We found other problems regarding how your bank manages the right-of-rescission disclosure process," she continued. "We noted on several instances, the borrower was not given the disclosures at the proper time during the application process."

The right of rescission is one of the craziest ideas contained within banking regulations. It centers around the premise that people who borrow money using their home as collateral don't realize they could lose their home to foreclosure in the event they default on the loan. The right of rescission restricts the bank from funding the loan until three days after borrowers sign the loan documents. The government believes that borrowers need additional time to mull this over, as if the consideration never entered their minds when they applied for the loan. Adding to the insanity, the law does not give borrowers the right to waive this waiting period.

"I've been in banking for about forty years," I responded. "I have never had a borrower exercise his or her right of rescission. In discussions with other bankers, I have never heard of a single instance where anyone has actually exercised their right of rescission. I know of numerous instances, however, where borrowers were incensed by the fact the regulation required them to wait for three days after loan closing before the loan could be funded. Do either of your colleagues know of an instance wherein a borrower actually exercised their right of rescission?"

Both of the other examiners shook their heads.

"How can we get so concerned about whether the timing of the disclosures was exactly right if the ROR is never going to be exercised anyway?"

Again, I had probably won the battle but lost the war. The examiners did not want commonsense responses, which was understandable, given that not much about government compliance lies within the realm of common sense. The atmosphere in the room was becoming decidedly chillier.

Undaunted, Ms. Ortega pulled out another report from her file. "Your Home Mortgage Disclosure Act reports are a mess. The bank has been using outdated software, which is no longer adequate. Our team was unable to tell from your data collection process whether or not the bank is engaging in any discriminatory practices. As your market area is approximately 45 percent Hispanic, we are particularly concerned about discriminatory practices toward Hispanic customers."

Speaking in Spanish, I asked her why she suspected we would want to discriminate against almost half our customer base. She interrupted me. "I don't speak Spanish. You need to respond in English."

"Okay," I replied, switching back to English, "I want to know why you think a bank in an area where 45 percent of the customer base is Hispanic would want to engage in discriminatory practices against Hispanics. We wouldn't be in business very long if the Hispanics in town thought were discriminating against them. Two of our five directors have Hispanic surnames. Both Nick and I, who aren't Hispanic, became fluent in Spanish so we could take better care of our Spanish-speaking customers. I find it somewhat ironic that although you haven't bothered to learn Spanish, you could be suspicious of people who have at least made the effort to learn the language. Seems to me, we try harder than you do."

Ms. Ortega was not amused. "Your ability to speak Spanish does not offset sloppy HMDA data. Again, Mr. Goodman, let me remind you of the seriousness of these matters. These regulations are the law, and as regulators, we expect and demand your full compliance with them.

"The final issue I want to bring to your attention is a gross instance of noncompliance with flood insurance requirements. As you know, we direct special attention to examining loans made by the bank to any of the bank directors. In our review of a loan the bank made to Dina Cervantes and her husband last fall, we noticed that although a picture of the property from the appraisal report clearly indicated there was a building on the property, the bank did not obtain flood insurance. The same appraisal report indicates said property is in a designated flood zone. This error has the appearance of being particularly serious because it appears the bank is granting favoritism to a director by not requiring this director to pay for flood insurance. In order to avoid a fine, I strongly suggest you obtain flood insurance on this property as soon as possible." She had pulled herself up to her full height, shaking her head in righteous indignation.

Dina was in the process of standing up, smoke coming out of her ears, when I motioned for her to stay seated.

"Ms. Ortega, I know you are desperately trying to get a scalp for your belt, but this is a poor battle to pick. Mrs. Cervantes and her husband own an equipment dealership. The property you are referring to is next to their facility. When it came up for sale, they decided to buy it, to use for their used equipment lot. The property had an old building on it. They removed the building immediately after completing the purchase of the property. At the time of the appraisal, the building was still standing and thus appeared in the appraiser's pictures of the property. They paid for most of the purchase in cash. The amount they borrowed was equal to about 25 percent of the appraised value. The building was given no value in the appraisal. Are you telling me they should have purchased flood insurance on a building they were going to tear down?"

"The regulation requires that flood insurance on all structures be in place at the time of closing," she replied. "I need a commitment from you to get the insurance in place as soon as possible."

Nodding seriously, I countered, "I'll get right on that. But tell me, how does one go about getting insurance on a building that is no longer there?"

She didn't have an answer. Nick and my two board members were shaking their heads in amazement as Ms. Ortega took her seat.

Mars regained control of the meeting. "This bank is very strong with regard to safety and soundness concerns. However, it is clear to me after listening to your responses that the bank does not exhibit the right attitude toward regulatory compliance. There has been an obvious lack of commitment of resources in the compliance area. You have only one compliance officer. He also performs other duties besides compliance. Your procedures are inadequate. Your hardware and software are grossly inadequate.

"In anticipation of this meeting, my staff and I developed a plan detailing the steps we want to see this bank take toward improving the compliance function. Though we will not issue sanctions or fines at this time, we fully expect to see marked improvement when we return for next year's examination. In the meantime, I will expect periodic reports on your progress."

The next hour of the meeting was a review of the plan Mars and her team had devised. I knew enough to just shut up and listen.

After they left, we all looked at each other in open amazement. "I can't believe they want to give so much grief to a bank like ours, which is obviously in no danger of failing," Fletcher snorted. "Seems to me the taxpayers would be much better served if the examiners spent most of their time trying to keep the marginal banks from going under, instead of tilting at windmills like this." Looking directly at me, he continued. "As the chairman of the board, I am directing you and Nick to look into the cost of making the changes the examiners have required. I don't know what we are going to do. Depending on the cost, we may have to raise more capital, sell the bank, merge with a bigger bank ... who the hell knows?"

On that sober note, the meeting mercifully was adjourned.

Saturday passed with the weight of Friday's meeting pressing down on my spirits. I had always tried to comply with the regulations, even when I considered them onerous, unfair, and detrimental to the people depending on the bank. I had a hard time paying attention to the homily Sunday morning as well. I couldn't keep my mind from scrolling back to the closeout session with the examiners or leaping forward to the round of golf with Herb scheduled for the afternoon. The former was depressing and anxiety-producing, but the latter prospect helped chase the darkness away.

After Mass ended—it was a Catholic Church weekend for Sheila and me—I shook hands at the door with our old Irish priest, Father John McKnorr, making my standard remark about how tough it must be to keep his flock from backsliding. He gave me his usual wide smile, along with his canned response. "Aye, Joe, my job would be much easier if the devil didn't have such a keen appetite for mutton." We both chuckled as he turned to shake hands with the next departing parishioner.

Sheila and I drove home. I was unusually silent.

"What's the matter, Joe?" she asked.

"I told you. The bank examiners are giving us a load of crap."

Sheila shook her head and sighed. "I know how they get under your skin. Don't let them get to you. It's not worth it."

"It's going to screw up my golf game—the pressure, I mean."

"Only if you let it."

"You sound like Herb."

Sheila laughed. I'd always loved the sound of her laugh. It cheered me up.

"I don't think that's true, Joe, but if you want to say so, that's fine."

We arrived home. I ate a light lunch, kissed Sheila good-bye, and drove to Herb's to pick him up. He was waiting for me on his porch. Tootie was curled up on one of the old rockers. He gave her a pat as he got up to leave. She wagged her tail lazily in response. It was hard to tell whether she was disappointed to be left behind or grateful to be left alone with an opportunity to catch up on her beauty rest.

Herb was never one to waste a minute. As soon as we pulled out of the driveway, he began explaining what we were doing and how it fit into the big picture.

"The reason I needed to find a course with very few players is that today you are going to be playing a one-man, four-ball scramble. This wouldn't be allowable under normal course traffic. The four-ball format, with you hitting four shots from each location, should give us a pretty good look at where your golf game is now, as well as a sense of your potential."

We arrived at the Hemphill course and went into the pro shop to register. Connell Thomas greeted us warmly. "Herb, it's been too long. The wife and I were just talking about asking you over for dinner sometime soon. Tell you what—if you promise to bring some of that herbal tea of yours, I'll waive the green fees for your friend today. My wife actually believes your tea makes me smarter."

"Well, it couldn't hurt any. Mentally, you have a whole lot more potential for upward movement than downward," Herb replied, laughing as he slapped his old friend on the shoulder. "Do you want us to start on the front or the back?"

"If you don't mind, start on the back. There are a couple of groups about to go off the front. The back is empty. By the time you make the turn, I don't believe anybody will be left on the front. Almost all my members played in the tournament this morning." He looked at me and winked. "Be careful with this old coot; he will try to teach you more than you really want to know.

"Give me a minute. You're going to need a cart if you want to finish before dark. I need to call Albert down at the cart barn to bring a cart that's fully charged. We used most of them for the tournament this morning."

It took only a couple of minutes for Albert to bring our cart. We strapped my bag on the back and drove to the tenth tee. Herb said he usually preferred to walk, but it would take too much time to chase all the balls on foot with the four-ball format.

The tenth hole at Hemphill Country Club was a relatively easy, straightaway par four. The tee was elevated, making the hole play shorter than the 410 yards shown on the scorecard. After some stretching exercises and numerous practice swings, I took four balls out of my bag and teed the first one between the markers. I was still a little stiff from the car ride, and my first shot was a weak slice that settled in the rough behind a group of trees. I improved with each of the subsequent three shots. The fourth was a nice 260-yarder, splitting the fairway.

My first two approach shots were poor. The third finished within ten feet of the cup. The round continued in much the same fashion, with my first shot usually being the worst of the four and either my third or my fourth shot being the pick of the litter.

At the turn, I bought soft drinks and sandwiches before heading for the first tee. My best ball score on the back was a four-under par thirty-two, not unusual for the format we were using. I did better on the front, no doubt becoming more adept at dealing with the "pressure" of playing my first round with Herb. I shot thirty, for an eighteen-hole score of sixty-two. We stopped at the pro shop to thank Connell for his hospitality before loading my clubs into the car for the ride home.

Herb was silent for the first few miles, apparently gathering his thoughts.

"Okay," he finally said, "let's examine what we learned today. It appears to me, your assessment of the present state of your golf game is pretty accurate. Judging from how you played your first shots, I would guess you would have scored about eighty-five if you had used only the first ball. The sixty-two you scored using your best shot each time gives us a glimpse of your potential. This scramble score may be somewhat of a false-positive since in the four-ball format it is typical to hit every green. This eliminated chipping and pitching, which are the weakest parts of your game. However, it's not a bad measuring stick."

I eased around a slow-moving tractor on the road in front of us. I knew the driver and waved. He waved back.

"I like the idea of potential," I said. "Gives me hope of doing better."

"Good!" Herb slapped both thighs with his hands.

"Don't get too excited, Herb!"

I glanced over at Herb and saw he was staring at me with a big grin on his face.

"Remember when we talked about the hypothetical situation of having a pro and a high handicapper hit balls to the same target all day?" he asked.

"Yeah, of course I do!"

"Well, this four-ball format relates to your ability to focus. My plan is to have you continue to play the scramble format, gradually working down to three balls, then two, and finally to the point where your focus is so strong that you shoot close to your scramble score using only one ball. We are going to give you an advantage over the vast majority of the Masters field, with regard to your ability to focus."

Herb went silent again and then asked, "Speaking of focus, anything wrong, Joe? I sensed you were struggling with your focus."

I told him about the bank examiners. His face went serious on me as he stared straight ahead.

"You've got to control your anxiety," he said.

"Easy for you to say."

"No, it's hard for me to say because I know how you hate bank examiners."

"I never said I hate bank examiners," I said, feeling the frustration well up inside me.

"You didn't have to. I can see how they've gotten to you. Cut it out, Joe! I mean, you did okay today, but I could tell there was something off."

"Sorry."

"No problem," Herb said. "Hey, let's lighten up a little, okay? So where was I?"

"You were talking about my potential."

"I think we'd moved on from that, but it doesn't matter. So we will also develop the conviction there is no such thing as pressure. That's really important!"

"I get it, Herb! You've said so a zillion times."

Ignoring me, Herb said, "I estimate most touring pros are about two- or three-handicappers with regard to their ability to focus and deal with their concept of pressure. The reason they break par so frequently is that their swing mechanics and touch are considerably better than scratch. We are going to build your mental game to the point where you will have a several-shot advantage over even the best pros with regard to running your brain. My goal is to take you to the point that you stand over every shot fully confident, unconcerned about any possible negative results."

"If you say so," I said morosely.

"Don't forget who you're working for!" Herb said.

"Uh-huh," I said.

We arrived back at Herb's a short time later. I dropped Herb off at his porch, leaving him to deal with Tootie. She met him with her supper bowl in her mouth and reproach in her eyes.

As I drove home, I thought about everything Herb had told me since we'd met. He was right about pressure and negativity. The bank examiners were part of doing business. Regulations were part of doing business. Why fight it and feel angry? I was soon filled with excitement as I thought maybe I could at last get a handle on how I dealt with all kinds of pressure. Obviously, judging from my scramble score, there was a guy who was a very good golfer somewhere inside me. I just needed to trust Herb's ability to bring this guy to the surface on every shot.

CHAPTER 5

HERB WAS TRUE TO HIS WORD. WE WORKED DOGGEDLY TOGETHER for the next six weeks, and my game steadily improved. Sheila commented that I was looking a bit leaner and that I had a sparkle in my eye that hadn't been there before. All good things! I'd even become better able to manage my brain, as Herb put it. I still occasionally gave in to pressure, especially at work, but I was getting better at dealing with it. At about this time, with summer having almost arrived, our full board of directors met to discuss plans for bringing the bank into compliance with the mandated requirements.

Along with Fletcher and Dina, our other three directors—Gilbert Gonzalez, Mike Currier, and Norman Berruti—were in attendance.

Responding to Fletcher's directive, my staff and I had laboriously gathered as much information as we could. Early in the process it had become obvious we would need outside help. I retained the services of Banker's Regcomp Inc., a small out-of-state consulting firm that supplied consultants who specialized in helping banks with regulatory compliance issues.

I opened the meeting with an introduction of Oscar Raymo, a senior partner at Regcomp. Mr. Raymo supplied each of us with a folder of information and began his PowerPoint presentation. "The good news is your examiners appear to know this isn't going to happen overnight. They've given you until your next review to make significant progress. The bad news is they unilaterally decide what constitutes significant progress." The board chuckled slightly at his attempt at gallows humor. He pressed on, taking about an hour to outline the steps we needed to take. When he provided his estimate of the total cost for the project, the entire board let out a gasp of disbelief.

"Good grief!" Fletcher responded. "That's roughly two years of our net earnings!"

Fletcher's assessment was dead-on. Although our little bank had almost always been profitable, our primary mission had been to provide reasonably priced banking services to our community. I don't know how many times I had heard Wally say, "You can shear a sheep many times, but you can skin it only once." This was his simple way of stating the fact that in order for the bank to stay in business, we had to help our customers stay in business.

"Looks to me like we are pretty well going to have to ask our shareholders to give up any dividends for at least two years if we want to pay for all of this out of earnings," Fletcher mused. "Either that, or we look at selling or merging the bank."

"I could never go along with selling to a large bank—or merging with one of them," Currier fumed. "They are no good for a town like ours. Let me tell you a little story. I am the finance chairman at my church. Five years ago, the church needed to borrow a sizable sum of money to pay for a large remodeling project. This was before I came onto the finance committee. One of the committee members at the time had a nephew who worked for a mega bank. He contacted his nephew and found out the mega bank had a special church-lending division. The church committee negotiated a loan from the mega bank, at what appeared to be very favorable terms. At least that's what they thought, until they came to the end of the first five-year renewal period for the loan. The committee had been led to believe that the renewals every five years were really just a formality, and the loan would continue to be rewritten on very friendly terms. Boy, did they get a shock! The mega bank offered them very onerous terms and threatened to invoke severe penalties if the church couldn't either pay the loan off in full or refinance with another lender before the call date. The bank didn't let them know about this until it was too late to arrange to refinance with another bank, so the church was trapped into a crummy deal. If a mega bank would be so heavy-handed with a church, can you imagine how they would treat our small businesses? Old Wallace Matthews would be turning over in his grave if we let that happen to our community."

The board continued discussing the ramifications of each alternative. After another hour, I was directed to contact our major stockholders to determine their reaction to forgoing dividends for at least two years. This did not sit very well with me because a good number of these stockholders were elderly and depended on their stock dividends to supplement their retirement. The board also directed me to explore merger possibilities. We thanked Mr. Raymo for his help and adjourned the meeting.

By early June, my golf game had improved even more. Despite the negativity at work, I was able to continue on an even keel brain-wise. God had sent me no additional e-mails. In a strange sort of way, I missed them! I asked Herb about this one day as we practiced, still using the scramble rounds to hone my ability to focus on each shot.

"Haven't heard from God," I said, trying to sound casual.

"That so?" Herb said, his voice as casual as mine.

"Yeah, He's been MIA since our first contact."

Herb snorted. "God's never MIA, Joe!"

"You know what I mean."

"Just 'cause you can't see Him doesn't mean He's not there."

I teed up. "Forget I asked."

"He's keeping an eye on you," Herb said. "Don't you worry!"

I never brought up the subject again. Instead, I concentrated on my early morning meditation periods, finding that they were key to the improvement in my mental game. I had gradually learned to focus intently during the brief time it took to execute a shot and then turn that focus off until the next shot. The improved ability to focus allowed me to score approximately the same with three balls as I had previously scored with four. More importantly, we estimated that my first-ball scores were close to even par. We spent endless hours working on my short game, specifically on distance control with wedge shots and short putting technique. Herb had identified these areas as my major weaknesses. He put grips on my wedges with colored bands similar to the Hotch woods. The bands created three precise grip positions on each wedge.

We practiced hitting wedge shots with half, three-quarter, and full swings with each wedge, using the different grip positions. We measured the distances produced by each variation. This information was put on a chart to use during play. It was amazing how much my wedge play improved. I knew, for instance, that if I had a shot of eighty-seven yards, I could fly it high, using my lob wedge at full grip, employing a full swing, or I could fly it low, using my pitching wedge at full choke with a half swing. My scores rapidly went down as a result of the improvement in my distance control.

Herb taught me his "yip-proof" method for making short putts. He called it body-putting. The method eliminated arm, wrist, and hand action. The simple stroke involved gripping the putter firmly in a neutral position, with the edges of the putter grip in the lifelines of each hand, and anchoring my elbows against my side. From this position I moved the putter by rocking my weight off the instep of my left foot for a backswing and then back onto the left instep for the downswing. Herb incorporated a drill, placing balls in a three-foot circle around the hole. I was not allowed to quit until I made fifty in a row. As I got close to fifty, the nervousness became similar to the kind I would feel in a tournament situation. Learning to confidently focus on my routine and technique as I approached the last few of the fifty putts was great mental practice as well as mechanical putting practice.

The most challenging parts of the process for me were the early morning meditation and exercise sessions. I was indeed concentrating on them and making progress, but the going wasn't easy. I suppose nothing worth achieving ever is easy, though it might be nice sometimes if it were. Anyway, it took a lot of discipline to turn off the TV and go to bed by nine o'clock every night. There were numerous times when the alarm went off at four that I wanted to roll over and go back to sleep. Following Herb's instructions, the meditation sessions consisted of my becoming completely relaxed and turning my brain off. Once I achieved a state of being as thought-free as possible, I began visualizing myself as a championship golfer—poised, confident, and playing effortlessly.

The aches and pains from the exercise sessions confirmed the old adage that "getting old isn't for sissies." My willpower was tested severely as I forced myself to do the strength and stretching exercises. It really helped that soon I was able to see measurable improvement in my strength and flexibility. As the weeks went by, my physical improvement translated into greatly improved club head speed. My drives were going at least twenty-five yards farther than when I had first starting working with Herb.

He thought winning my local club championship would be an excellent shortcut toward establishing a handicap low enough to qualify as a participant in the Mid-Amateur, so we both moved toward that objective.

Our head professional, Marty Clute, was flabbergasted when I walked into his shop to register for the club championship. It had been several years since I had played competitive golf. I was no longer considered a serious player. I hadn't even bothered to turn in enough scores to establish a handicap. Marty was no fool when it came to assessing golf talent. He had been an excellent player in his prime, qualifying for the professional tour right out of college. He'd had fair success as a tour player, until he damaged both wrists in a motorcycle accident, ending his ability to compete at a high level. Although he seemed content with the life of a small-town home pro, I suspected he regretted the sudden end to his playing career.

"Joe," Marty told me, shaking his head, "the only way you can play in the club championship is for me to put you in the championship flight. It is the only flight played at scratch, so not having a handicap doesn't matter. I'm guessing you will be twenty years older than anyone in the flight. I would have to place you as the lowest seed, which means you would be playing our defending champion, Derek Finucane, in the first round. Are you sure you want to do this?"

"Perfect," I replied. "If I get clobbered in the first match, it will free up the rest of my weekend for some yard work Sheila has been nagging at me to get done. Is it still the same format, with sixteen players in the flight—winner has to win four matches over two days?"

"We've never changed it, even though it's been hard to get sixteen guys who want to play at scratch, especially with Derek in the flight. He has won it four or five years in a row. Almost never has a close match. Wins at least five up with four to go most of the time."

I knew Derek and his family fairly well. Twenty years ago, I had been his Little League baseball coach. His father and I had played regularly when I was a serious golfer. Derek was a gifted athlete. He had excelled in football and basketball in high school. After graduating, he'd received a full-ride scholarship to play football at a small out-of-state college. But things didn't work out for him at college. He returned after three years. His father owned a successful insurance agency and took him into the business. Derek developed an obsession with golf, spending the kind of time on the course only a boss's son could afford. He had an attractive wife he had married at college and two adorable kids. I almost never saw him with them. He was always at the golf course, leaving the kids' activities for his wife to handle.

Herb and I worked extra hard before the tournament, fine-tuning my short shots and preshot routine. We made a recording for me to incorporate into my morning meditations. The recording featured positive affirmations to sharpen my ability to focus on each shot as well as strengthen my faith. I gradually became more and more confident.

Regardless of the vast improvements in my game and in my brain management, I was still a bit nervous when the day of the club championship arrived. The opening round would be the first official test of my progress since Herb had started working with me in April.

After checking in at the pro shop, Herb and I headed for the range with a small bucket of balls. He reminded me to just concentrate on rhythm and relaxation.

"Twenty minutes before you play a tournament round is no time to give yourself a lesson," he advised. "Just get into a confident rhythm and forget about mechanics. Don't worry if you mishit a few of the range balls. Pick small targets and focus on them."

Halfway through the bucket, I told Herb I was feeling about as relaxed and confident as possible. We decided to leave the range and hit a few chips and putts at the practice green. "Same thing here," Herb interjected. "Don't worry about making any putts. Just concentrate on smoothing out your stroke and getting a feel for the speed of the green."

My opponent had not appeared. I had noticed his car in the parking lot when I arrived. Apparently, he had elected to have breakfast in the club dining room, figuring he would not need to warm up to dispatch me. Hard to argue with his thinking, since no one had given him a close match in several years, and I was the lowest seed in the flight.

The old speaker box outside the pro shop door sputtered. "Five-minute call for the first match in the Championship Flight. Derek Finucane and Joe Goodman, you've got the tee."

Herb and I were chatting with the starter when Derek came roaring up in a golf cart. He appeared upset when he saw I was walking with a caddy. I presumed he would have preferred we both take a cart. In that case, the match would be over much faster, and he would have more time to prepare for his next match, which would likely be against a much more worthy opponent than me. He was polite enough not to say anything, but plainly, he was unhappy.

The first hole was a very simple par five. The only obstacle was a small creek that crossed the fairway just in front of the green. I had the honor. Derek raised an eyebrow when he noticed I was using my slice Hotch rather than a driver. This strategy was a product of Herb's golf intelligence. Because I had no intention of going for the green in two, I might as well lay up from the tee, giving myself a better chance of hitting the fairway. I teed my ball and made a relaxed swing. The result was a modest 220 yards, slightly to the right of the middle of the fairway.

Derek snorted at my shot and took a few hard practice swings with his driver. He teed the ball high and took a vicious rip at it. The ball flew almost one hundred yards past mine, missing the fairway by about ten yards to the left.

Herb and I ambled down the fairway as Derek jumped into his cart and barreled by us. "I don't believe in using gamesmanship to gain an advantage over an opponent," Herb said as we were approaching my ball. "But Derek is going to go crazy waiting on us if he jumps into his cart and speeds to his ball like that every time."

We chose a five-iron for our second shot, calculating that it would leave a third shot of approximately 110 yards, one of my most accurate distances. Our strategy also took the creek completely out of play. The shot came off exactly as planned, leaving my ball on a good lie in the fairway.

Derek surveyed his lie. It wasn't good. But nevertheless, he chose to go for the green. He selected a three-iron for the shot. Bad choice. A three-iron from a scruffy lie is not easy for your second shot of the day, particularly when you haven't hit any warm-up shots. He half-skulled the shot, sending it on a low line drive into the creek.

We estimated my third shot to be 112 yards to the pin, pretty much a stock pitching wedge for me. With Herb's encouragement, I went through my preshot routine and hit an almost perfect approach. It spun to a stop within a foot of the hole.

Derek's ball was partially submerged in a small ripple of water along the edge of the creek. In a game effort to salvage the hole, he took a stance in the creek and tried to muscle the ball onto the green with a savage explosion shot. His effort moved a large amount of water and mud, much of which settled on his clothing. The ball landed on the opposite side and insolently spun back into the creek.

Wisely, he didn't try to retrieve his ball. Motioning at me to pick up my ball, he conceded the hole.

The second hole was one of those cute little par threes often found on non-championship-caliber courses. Measuring only 105 yards, the green's primary defense was its quirky slope from back to front. I still had the honor, which gave Derek time to clean most of the mud from his shoes and pants.

"Okay, let's be smart here," Herb whispered. "Last thing we need to do is leave a downhill putt on this screwy little green. Choke your pitching wedge halfway down, and swing easy. I don't think you can hit it past the hole with the choked wedge."

Following Herb's instructions, I hit a respectable shot that landed ten feet on the front of the green and backed off to the front collar. I was left with about twenty-five feet, straight uphill to the cup.

Derek's temperament was not compatible with playing a delicate wedge shot. In addition to losing the first hole to an old man, he had added insult to injury by ruining his favorite golf pants. I was sure he knew he was going to catch hell from his friends when he trooped back into the clubhouse, looking more like he had been in a mud-wrestling contest than in a golf match. He selected his sand wedge, apparently intending to fly the ball well past the hole and spin it back for an easy uphill putt. His execution was almost perfect. The ball landed twelve feet above the hole. Unfortunately for him, it didn't spin back. In his frustration over his failed explosion from the creek, he had neglected to clean the mud from the grooves of his sand wedge, merely wiping the club with his towel before turning attention to his pants. As a result, the ball hit the green with no backspin and settled about two feet above its landing point. He stared at it in disbelief. It took a moment for him to figure out what had happened. He sat in his golf cart fuming for a few minutes as he painstakingly cleaned the wedge's grooves with the point of a golf tee.

I played my simple second shot well, leaving the ball at the edge of the hole for an easy par. Derek had little chance to two-putt. His first putt, though hit softly, trickled eight feet past the hole. He rimmed out his comebacker.

The match settled into an easy pattern for me. Following Herb's advice, I focused intensely on each shot. He had a steady supply of jokes and questions that took my mind completely away from golf between shots. We continued to play conservative shots, never leaving Derek an open opportunity. Obviously shaken by the first two holes, he became more and more frustrated with my steady performance and the time it took for Herb and me to walk the course. He had clearly succumbed to his own self-generated pressure, imagining defeat at the hands of someone like me. This resulted in poor decisions and rushed swings. He failed to win a hole. I closed him out two down with one to go.

Herb was ecstatic, pounding my back happily as we walked off the sixteenth green. I couldn't help but feel empathy for Derek. This same sort of embarrassment had led me to quit competitive golf years ago. As I walked over to shake his hand, I swore I could see tears in his eyes. A soft breeze blew over the course, redolent with the smell of freshly mown grass. The sky was a brilliant blue. The day had been perfect for me, but I knew it hadn't been for Derek. His hand felt cold and clammy when we shook. "Thanks for the game," I said, smiling sympathetically.

"Sure, Joe," Derek mumbled, looking down at his muddy shoes.

It was a long-standing tradition of our club championship for the winner of a match to buy a drink for the loser afterward. "Say, I need to get home and finish some yard work. Instead of my buying you a drink at the clubhouse, would it be all right if I met you later at the Farmhouse Beer Palace for a drink?" I asked, knowing he'd probably jump at the chance to avoid being paraded as the match loser in front of his friends.

His face lit up. "That would be great, Joe! How about six?" he replied.

I agreed to six, and Derek shook my hand again before trudging off to his car.

CHAPTER 6

‖‖

A T THE END OF THE DAY, I DROPPED HERB OFF AT HIS PLACE, promising I wouldn't indulge in more than one beer with Derek. As I drove to the Farmhouse Beer Palace, I thought about the matches I'd played earlier. I was pleased. Very pleased!

I pulled into the parking lot. A minute or so later, I walked through the back door of the bar. It was a little after six. Pausing to let my eyes adjust to the dim light, I realized how exhausted I was. It had been a long time since I had played two rounds of golf in one day. Herb and I had used a cart for the second round to conserve our energy. Even so, I had spent a lot of time out in the sun.

My second-round opponent was the pro's son, Mickey Clute. He gave me an unexpected edge. His opponent for the first round had been his brother-in-law, Larry Brown. Their postround traditional beer had escalated into a six-pack, and he arrived at the first tee a little tipsy. By the time he sobered up, I had him four down and went on to win, three and two. I offered to buy him a beer after our match, but he begged off, telling me he still had a headache from the aftermath of consoling his brother-in-law.

At the Farmhouse, my eyes gradually adjusted, and I spotted Derek by himself in a corner booth. He was dressed in a sports shirt and jeans, similar to most of the guys in the place. His decision to start without me was evidenced by two empty cans on the table.

I caught a waitress en route with his third beer. I asked her to turn

61

around and get one for me and said that I would pay for both. She nodded and made a U-turn toward the bar.

"Sorry I'm a little late," I said. "Had to drop Herb off before heading over here."

Derek looked at me, his face sad, as I sat down. "You played well today, Joe," he said.

"Thanks," I said. "I wouldn't worry about the outcome. Everybody's going to have an off day."

"Yeah, I suppose so," Derek said.

"Looks like you've made yourself at home while you were waiting for me," I said.

"Might as well," he replied, shaking his head. "This place has become like home to me since Sharon kicked me out a couple of weeks ago. Most people don't know about it yet. I've been staying in a little apartment across the street."

"Darn, Derek, sorry to hear about that," I said. "Anything I can do to help?"

"I really need somebody to talk to—or, hell, maybe some therapy. My dad always told me you were about the most levelheaded guy he'd ever met. You were my favorite coach back in Little League. You always seemed to care more about helping us kids than about winning. Maybe you can help me get my head screwed on right again."

I leaned back in my chair. The guy didn't look so good. He really didn't. I was a little worried about him, what with the news he'd just shared. I hadn't heard about him and Sharon.

"I can try, Derek. Sheila says I'm usually a good listener."

And then Derek launched into his story. He really did seem to need to talk.

"For the past several months, I have been sinking into, I guess, some form of depression. I didn't succeed in college like everybody thought I would. Now I'm back in town working for my dad. I don't give a damn about the insurance business, but what else could I do? I'm thirty years old, and it's almost like I never grew up. I don't feel like I'm accomplishing anything. About the only thing I felt good about was my golf game. Now you've managed to take that away." Obviously embarrassed at this confession, he stared at the table, drawing little circles with his beer can. The waitress came with our beers. I thanked her and paid the tab.

"Derek, look me in the eye. I'm going to give you a little butt-kicking here. I've worried for years that you were spending too much time at the club and not enough time with your family. You've become the poster child for what can be bad about golf. Golf can provide a wonderful opportunity for parents to interact with their kids. On the other hand, it can also be an ugly four-letter word, family-wise, when it takes a guy away from his wife and kids. You have chosen the ugly option."

Derek crushed his beer can.

"My beating you today is probably the best thing that could have happened for you," I continued. "If we weren't sitting in a redneck bar, I would call it an epiphany, but under these circumstances, let's go with 'wake-up call.'

"First of all, realize how lucky you are. You are experiencing something akin to a midlife crisis at the age of thirty, instead of waiting until you are fifty. By fifty, you would have wasted much of your life and hurt people you care about, and it would be too late to change a heck of a lot. At thirty, you can make major corrections in your course before you do much permanent damage. You are not a stupid guy. Tell me how it could be more important to be the best golfer in a small town than to be a great husband and father. Are a bunch of silly-ass trophies more important than your wife and kids? You only get one chance for your kids to grow up thinking they've got the best dad in the world. You don't get a mulligan. Just as bad, if your kids don't see a good example in parenting from you, the results will show up in your grandkids as well."

He nodded, tears welling up in his eyes. "God, Joe. You don't pull punches, do you? Just wanted to talk. I didn't expect this little trip to the woodshed. Two weeks ago, I would have told you that you were full of crap. Sitting alone in that apartment at night has led me to do some serious reflecting about my life. But you … you're absolutely right. I have been looking at my life from only my own perspective—how it was affecting me, not considering Sharon and the kids. How do I turn things around?"

"First of all, you need to get out of this bar," I advised. "There is no problem that alcohol can't make worse. Also, a good-looking guy like you drunk in a bar late at night is bound to attract some gal on the make who knows how to manipulate drunks. You could wind up adding cheating on your wife to your other problems. Swallow your pride. Get out of here right now. Call Sharon. Tell her you've seen the light. Promise her that if she will take you back, things are going to be a whole lot different."

Derek didn't look convinced.

"Second step is to work on the crisis that put you in this mess. No good bringing it right back into the house with you."

"How do I do that?"

"I want to tell you a little trick I learned only a few months ago, which resulted in an incredible change in my life. Again, you're lucky. You will be getting a thirty-three-year head start on me with regard to this. It is extremely simple. I want you to change your concept of a day. Start going to bed at nine in the evening and waking up at four in the morning. Use the extra morning time to meditate and pray about what you want to do with the rest of your life. I guarantee an answer will come. As the answer starts to clarify, begin to use the time to focus on planning how to make it happen. Although your problem seems huge in your present state of mind, the solution is amazingly simple, if you will let God help you. You can't achieve goals unless you have goals. Right now, your primary goal should be to become the kind of husband and father your family deserves."

"You guarantee it will work? Who gave you this idea? How can you guarantee it?"

"I'll answer those questions the second week of April. Not going to tell you anymore until then. Just go on faith. It will probably take about twenty-one days before you start to see good results with the morning sessions. What do you have to lose? You are going to be three weeks older in twenty-one days, whether you do this or not."

We sat in silence for several minutes as Derek let my words soak in. I saw a change in his demeanor. An obvious glimmer of hope was forming in his eyes.

"Joe, I don't know why, but something tells me to trust you about this. Hell, as you say, I don't really have anything to lose but a little time, even if you're wrong. I've never even tried to put together a clear plan about what I want to achieve in my life. No wonder it has seemed so purposeless. You're right—the golf match today was a perfect wake-up call to make me see the light. I'm going to throw away my pride, just like I got rid of those muddy pants. It might take me a couple of weeks to start to figure things out and screw up enough courage to call Sharon." Derek rose from the booth. "Take care of the tip for me. That little waitress has been hitting on me the last couple of nights, and I don't want to give her any encouragement. She's never going to see me in this place again." He shook my hand and strode purposefully toward the exit.

Neither of us had touched the two beers. I gave them to a couple of young guys at the next booth and left out the back door. *Herb would be proud of my willpower,* I thought as I started my car.

After my two victories on Saturday, my confidence was at an all-time high. I became more comfortable and "tournament tough" with each match. Sunday, I defeated the high school golf coach, Charlie Johnson, two and one, in our morning semifinal match, and I won the final against Lou Henson on the first hole of sudden death, after I had tied the match with a birdie on the eighteenth hole. Lou was home from college for the summer. He was the best player on his college team and had been expected to be the strongest challenge for Derek.

I asked Herb if he wanted to stick around for the awards banquet. He declined, telling me he needed to get home to Tootie. "She was pretty darned upset with me last night," he explained. "Gave me a really disgusted look when I finally showed up to feed her. Hell hath no fury such as a dachshund scorned." He tried to look serious but couldn't pull it off. We were both a little giddy over our victory.

I took Herb home and swung by the house to pick up Sheila for the awards banquet. She didn't seem properly shocked about my success. "I must admit I had serious doubts. Dove or no dove, the whole thing seems pretty preposterous. But somehow, I just knew you were going to win," she said, giving me a hug. "Over the past few months you've seemed to be more positive about everything. You have an aura of success and confidence about you. It's like you have become a new and improved version of yourself."

Later in the evening, the club chairman presented me with the trophy. I was expected to give a little speech. Remembering what I had been told about keeping my mission a secret, I gave a trite little talk about never being too old to try and the importance of believing in yourself. My words probably didn't resonate very significantly with most of the club members, who by that time had been well overserved.

Marty Clute caught me as I was getting ready to leave. "The handicap committee had an impromptu meeting in the bar before the banquet," he reported. "We looked at your scorecards for the four tournament rounds. Did you know you were a total of ten under par for the holes you completed?"

I acknowledged I had not really been thinking about my medal score, so I wasn't aware of this.

"In addition," Marty continued, "you beat Derek, who is a plus-two handicap; Billy and Charlie, who are both scratch; and Lou, who is a fine college player. In view of your performance, we are going to assign you an official handicap of scratch."

Scratch, an official handicap of zero, would serve me well.

"That's fine with me Marty," I replied. "Kind of like a battlefield promotion. I honestly didn't know what to expect from myself. I agree with the committee's decision. I don't want people to think I am some sort of a sandbagger."

Driving home, I couldn't keep the smile off my face. Herb had been right. Thanks to his plan, in the space of one weekend, I had gone from not having an established handicap to having an official handicap low enough to qualify for the Mid-Amateur.

My practice sessions with Herb continued. You might say we'd fallen into a comfortable routine. We'd become close friends in many ways. We didn't finish each other's sentences or anything, but we just had that comfortable relationship that comes with trust and giving the other person the space he needs. I still hadn't heard from God again, and I sometimes wondered whether the whole thing had been a figment of an overworked mind, but there was something about Herb that made me believe he was with me for a reason. I just kept the faith and kept right on moving toward the goal.

The Fourth of July weekend came and went, and I was sitting in my office on Monday morning worrying about a scheduling conflict. I had registered my entry into the Mid-Amateur Tournament the week following my victory in the club championship. The Mid-Amateur was scheduled for the week of September 8, the exact date of our state banking association's annual conference. As the incoming president of the association, I was expected to attend the conference. The members of my board were also planning to attend.

As I sat pondering my dilemma, an e-mail from the state banking association popped up in my inbox. The e-mail read, "Due to delays with our host hotel's remodeling project, the hotel has asked us to reschedule our meeting to the week of September 15. We apologize for any inconvenience to our members. It would be impossible for us to rebook another hotel at this late date. We have no choice but to change our meeting date to the week of September 15."

"What a coincidence! What a lucky break!" I whooped, standing and applauding my computer monitor.

A new window suddenly sprang to life on my computer screen. A message rapidly appeared in bold gold letters.

God is back! I thought, before reminding myself that God had never gone anywhere.

> *"Still believe in coincidences and luck, Joe? Here's your lesson for today: There are no coincidences. There is no such thing as good or bad luck. Everything happens for a reason. Here's another tidbit for you to absorb: Whenever a person fully commits to a righteous plan, unseen forces surface to help him or her along the way. Keep believing and working with Herb. I'll take care of the rest. By the way, congratulations on winning your club championship, but especially for the way you helped Derek."*

"I really feel good about that," I responded, typing frantically as I tried to keep up with the flood of words in my mind. "The Sunday after our little talk, I saw Derek in church with his family. First time I had seen him there with his family in years. They seemed very happy. The smaller of the girls was sitting in Derek's lap, and her older sister stood on the pew, hugging his neck. Sharon caught my eye and mouthed a 'thank you' to me just before Mass started.

"Derek stopped by the bank last week. He seemed like a different person. Couldn't wait to tell me about his early morning hours. He said it gradually came to him during his prayers and meditating that what he really wanted to do with his life was become a high school teacher and a coach. He had a long talk with his dad about it. His dad knew Derek's heart wasn't in the insurance business and was completely supportive of the idea. They are working out a plan for Derek to finish his degree.

"Derek told me, 'You won't see me on the golf course again, unless my family is playing with me. From now on, golf is going to bring me closer to my kids, not keep me from them.'

"Hey! I think I just felt a lightbulb go off. You are not at all surprised about this, are you? This was all part of my mission, wasn't it?"

> *"Even a banker will slowly catch on! As important as your mission is, it is not the only thing I have to worry about. I have to do a lot of juggling. At any given moment, I have an infinite number of balls in the air. Anytime I can kill two birds with one stone, I do it. Better not repeat the bird-killing analogy. It doesn't mix well with the old 'his eye is on the sparrow' concept.*
>
> *"You are doing fine. Just keep the faith and listen to Herb. Don't forget that I'm always around."*

The screen went blank.

Betti's voice crackled over the intercom. "Joe, Mary Garcia just walked in and asked if you have time to see her."

"I always have time for Mary. Please send her in."

Mary Garcia is one of my favorite people. I've known her since I was a kid. Her only son, Paul, was my best friend all through school. We were on the same Little League baseball team. Our high school team won the state championship when we were seniors. Paul played shortstop and was our most valuable player. I was barely better than average at second base.

Mary had been widowed for over ten years and was always strapped for cash. Well into her eighties, she was still taking in laundry to supplement her social security check. She had taken out loans from the bank several times over the years to meet emergencies and always paid back ahead of schedule.

She had been taking care of her great-granddaughter, Farrah, for the past two years. Paul, his wife, and their son and daughter-in-law had been killed in a car accident. They were hit by a drunk driver as they were returning from celebrating Farrah's fifth birthday at a restaurant down in the valley. Thank goodness Farrah was securely fastened in the car seat Sheila and I had given them for her baby shower. She escaped with only minor cuts and bruises.

I had been with them at the party. As usual, I had been giving Paul a hard time about his son being so obsessed with the *Charlie's Angels* television show that he had named his daughter after one of the show's stars. "It's a good thing they didn't have a boy," I teased, "or else he would have had to be tougher than the boy named Sue in that old Johnny Cash song." Paul smiled and gave me the finger, just like he had in high school every time I botched an easy grounder. "Bend your knees, gringo!" he would yell at me. I would give anything to have him still around, giving me the finger whenever I mess up.

"How's Farrah doing?" I asked as Mary entered and took a seat in front of my desk. I was almost afraid to ask. Farrah had developed a rare type of blood cancer. Her doctors weren't very hopeful.

"She still needs more treatment," Mary responded. "That's why I'm here to see about another loan." She handed me a completed loan application, which she had apparently picked up on an earlier trip to the bank. "I need another $8,000 to pay for her next treatments. As you know, the drunk who killed her grandparents and parents died at the scene." After pausing to make the sign of the cross, she continued. "He was an illegal immigrant with no insurance, so there were no funds to collect. We didn't have much insurance ourselves. We just never imagined anything like this happening."

I shook my head, wondering at the unfortunate circumstances. Paul and his son had operated a small nursery business that barely supported their families. Large life insurance policies were luxuries they couldn't afford.

"Joe, you know I don't have much in the way of collateral. The little insurance we had was just about enough to cover the funeral expenses. I sold Paul's home and mortgaged mine to get money for Farrah's treatments. That money is gone. My old car runs but isn't worth anything. I can afford to pay about $150 per month for this loan. You know I always pay my debts. See what you can do, *mijo*."

With that, she slowly raised her body out of the chair, gave me a warm hug, and left, waving at the tellers as she crossed through the lobby.

I sat at my desk, fiddling with my pen, trying to decide what to do. Years ago, I could have taken her circumstances into consideration and made her a loan that she could afford. Now, I couldn't. The government, in its infinite wisdom, now mandated that banks treat all customers alike. The reasoning was noble, in that the regulations were meant to eliminate discrimination, but like most well-intended attempts to control human behavior, other problems were created as unintended by-products. In cases like Mary's, the government had eliminated my bank's ability to lend with our heart.

I did some quick calculations. If I followed our required policy, Mary's payment would be $365/month, more than double what she had said she could afford. If I ignored policy and gave her special terms, I put the bank at risk of a fine for discrimination. It was beyond amazing that a small private business such as a community bank couldn't be given a little latitude to help people.

An idea popped into my head. I did some more calculations. I pushed the button on my intercom and asked Betti to come into my office. "Here's what we're going to do to help Mary," I told her as she settled into the chair just vacated by Mrs. Garcia. "I have a $10,000 personal certificate of deposit that doesn't mature until next year. If I pledge my certificate as collateral for Mary's loan, we can offer her the special rates applying to cash-secured loans. My quick calculation indicates her payment would work out to be $147 per month. Prepare the loan papers and call Mary to come in and sign.

"But whatever you do, do not let Mary know about my collateral pledge. It would greatly wound her pride if she knew I was doing this for her. Don't let anyone else in the bank know about this either, not even Leah in the collateral vault. Give the CD to her in a sealed envelope. It's a little bit awkward all the way around. I hope the examiners don't look at this closely. They might decide I am being discriminatory for loaning her the use of my certificate since I wouldn't do it for just anyone who walked through the door."

"Discriminatory?" said Betti. "Do you really think they'd see it that way?"

"Maybe," I said. "It has always been amazing to me, how our government is so concerned about banks having discriminatory practices while at the same time insurance companies are freely allowed to practice blanket discrimination with regard to how they set car insurance rates. Drivers under twenty-five years old are charged more than older drivers, teenage boys are charged more than teenage girls, and young single drivers are charged more than young married drivers, for example. If that isn't age and sex discrimination, I'll kiss a hog on the butt. But enough ranting. Please just do everything you can to keep anyone from finding out about what I'm doing for Mary."

"Mum's the word," Betti beamed. "And I don't mind telling you that you are one heck of a good guy."

As Betti exited my office, the printer started on its own. It spit out a single sheet of paper, with a single word printed in large gold letters:

"DITTO!"

In spite of the pat on the back I had received from God, I was disturbed about Mary's situation. I couldn't reconcile how the same God who was sending me on a mission of faith could allow tragedies such as those that had befallen Mary and her family. They were wonderful people; how could this have happened?

Later in the afternoon, Herb and I were practicing bunker shots. After several failures to get the ball out of the bunker, it was obvious that my focus had taken the afternoon off.

"Hold on, Joe," Herb said, climbing out of the bunker and sitting on the edge. "You obviously aren't into practicing today. You seem bothered. What's going on? Is Sheila unhappy with the time you're spending out here? She's bound to be feeling a little neglected."

"No. That's not it," I replied. "Sheila is mostly good with this. I can sense a little resentment at times, but she is basically on board." I told him about my visit earlier in the day with Mary Garcia and how it had led to my unsettling questions about God's priorities.

"Life is such that most people wrestle with these issues," Herb said, nodding. "We are all faced with trying circumstances that lead us to question our faith. Nobody gets out of this life without some scars. It has always helped me to think in terms of different perspectives, like the old analogy of an expensive Persian rug. If you saw only the underside of such a rug, it would seem like an ugly, random mess of lines and colors, without any beauty or logic. If you viewed the same rug from the top side, you would see the pattern and realize that all the mess on the other side had created a beautiful work of art. Maybe we just don't see the same side of the rug that God does."

"Hmm. There's some comfort in what you are telling me, but I guess it does just boil down to having faith, faith that God is in charge, and things will work out in the end. Thanks for the reminder, Herb. My mission and everything else—it's all just a question of faith, isn't it?"

Herb just grinned at me and told me to get my head screwed back on.

CHAPTER 7

||||||||||||||||||||||||||||||||||||||||||||||||||||||||||||||||||||||||||||||||||||||||||||||||||||||||||||||||||||||||||||||||||||||||||||||||||||||||||||||||||||||||||||||

AUTUMN GAVE WAY TO WINTER, LIKE IT ALWAYS DID, AND OUR little town geared up first for Thanksgiving and then for the Christmas holidays. A few days before Christmas, Herb and I were sitting by the small makeshift woodstove in his old mobile home in the early evening. A cold wind that had been blowing all afternoon continued to gently rock the little structure. A light snow began to fall. I was grateful for the cheery fire, along with the customary glass of homemade apple brandy Herb had supplied. "Brain tonic," he explained, to excuse these occasional departures from his no-alcohol policy. As the days shortened, we had shifted my training to working on short-game skills in Herb's barn, along with mental skills sessions in his small living room. This evening we had worked on some putting drills in the barn before retiring to the house for our nightly game of darts.

Months ago, before our first darts game, Herb had told me, "I don't want you to learn a damn thing about dart-throwing technique. Don't give a thought to how you hold the dart, whether you bend your elbow, how you stand, or anything about the physical aspect of dart throwing. I want you to just concentrate on the target and nothing else. This is all about learning to trust your instincts and natural ability. You'll be surprised how much it will help your golf game, especially your putting."

"Good thing you've never beaten me at darts," Herb warned this evening as he stroked the old dog on his lap. "Tootie roots for me. She's

75

not a very good sport. Might pee on your shoes if you ever won." At the sound of her name, Tootie briefly opened one eye, quickly discovered there was no food involved with her name reference, and went back to sleep. A world-class expert at relaxation, she had no need for the brandy's calming effect.

As crazy as the old coot had appeared at first, I had learned to trust Herb completely. Trusting him and having faith were the two primary instructions I had received at the start of the mission. Herb's observations were unfailingly reliable. Everything he told me worked. The combination of Herb's improvements to my golf technique and his on-course coaching was generating amazing results.

We had breezed through the Mid-Amateur in September. I played well enough in the preliminary medal competition to easily qualify for one of the sixty-four match play spots. Herb's coaching and my superior ability to focus more than made up for any lack of physical skill on my part. Before the final match, Herb told me to see myself as an actor who was playing the role of the world's greatest golfer. "Be poised and extremely confident," he advised. "The rest will take care of itself." I hardly recognized myself that day. I played at a level above anything I had previously experienced. I won three up, with a clinching birdie on the thirty-fourth hole of the final match. In the excitement following, everything became a blur. About the only thing I remembered afterward was some USGA official handing me the trophy and saying, "The best thing about this, Joe, is you're on your way to the Masters!"

As we sat in comfortable silence this December night, I watched the shadows from the fire play along Herb's bookcases. The time since we'd met had certainly been eventful. The mission had already created some good stuff, like with Derek and with Mary and Farrah.

Mary had invited Sheila and me over for dinner two weeks earlier. We were both apprehensive. No one had seen much of Farrah for several months. We were anticipating the worst, assuming Mary had asked us over in order for Tio Joe and Tia Sheila to offer comfort and say our last good-byes to the little girl.

We could not have been more wrong. As soon as Mary greeted us at the door, I could tell by the expression on her face that something wonderful was afoot. "I am so happy you could come," she beamed as she held the door for us. We were instantly immersed in the mouthwatering aromas of Mexican food simmering on the kitchen stove. Blending with the delightful smell was the sound of someone banging out a cheerful rendition of Beethoven's "Ode to Joy" on the piano upstairs.

"Who is playing that old piano of yours?" I asked, thinking it was one of Farrah's friends over for a visit.

"Who do you think, Joe?" Mary gushed. "It's Farrah, of course. Last summer she quit playing because she thought she was going to die. She told me it was no use practicing if she wasn't going to live long enough to become a great pianist. Now that she knows she isn't going to die, she practices all the time."

"She's getting better? That's wonderful news, Mary!" Sheila said.

"That's terrific!" I said.

"She's not just getting better," Mary said. "We think she is completely cured! Come. Sit down. We'll have a glass of sangria, and I'll tell you the story. My sauce needs to simmer for a few more minutes anyway."

Sheila and I plopped down on the living room couch. Mary scurried off to the kitchen and returned with a bottle of wine and three stemmed glasses. Sitting in an overstuffed chair across the coffee table from us, she carefully poured the wine and took a sip before settling into her story.

"I'm afraid I didn't tell you all the facts when I borrowed the $8,000 in July," she began. "At the time, the doctors were giving us no hope. Farrah's disease was steadily progressing. The doctors didn't think she had more than a few months left.

"Father McKnorr told me about a new experimental treatment being offered by a clinic in Santa Fe, New Mexico. I felt we had nothing to lose, so I called them. The man who answered the telephone was a retired Catholic priest who volunteers his time at the clinic. He told me the clinic does not charge for their treatments, which are completely funded by a very wealthy family whose child was cured at the clinic. He told me they specialize in treating patients who weren't responding to conventional treatments. The clinic's treatment is highly unconventional. It is a spiritual exercise based on a strong faith in the curative powers God has installed in our minds. These curative powers work primarily at the subconscious level. Most of the clinic's success has been with children. A childlike faith, uncommon in adults, is the key to success.

"The old priest was so sincere and positive. I decided this was Farrah's best chance to survive. The $8,000 I borrowed was for traveling expenses back and forth to Santa Fe.

"From the first day at the clinic, I knew we were on the right track. Every one of their staff was extremely positive and upbeat. They made Farrah feel as if she were the most special little girl in the world. Farrah was assigned her own individual caseworker. They call them 'angels' at the clinic. Her angel was Dionicia, who looked to be about my age but had more energy than one of those bunnies they use to advertise batteries on television. For the first two days all she did was get to know Farrah, playing with her for hours, talking about how important it was for her to truly believe she was going to get well. Dionicia discovered that Farrah dearly loves cats. Our old cat, Mamacita, has had two litters since Farrah has been living with me. Farrah loved helping me take care of the kittens. This information was critical to the treatment plan they developed for Farrah. They customize their approach for each child. Farrah's treatment was designed around cats. I'm not sure I understand it completely, but it involved a lot of visualization, along with some special virtual-reality technology they made just for Farrah."

"Virtual reality?" I interjected. "This sounds pretty far out there, Mary."

"You bet it was!" she replied, not the least perturbed by my interruption. "I didn't question it. At least we had something to cling to for hope. The people were so positive that it became very hard to doubt. They told us not to dwell on the technical part but to stay focused on having a strong, simple faith. Dionicia spent hours with Farrah, teaching her to visualize her bad blood cells as little rats and her good blood cells as protective cats attacking and eating the rats. When the rats were all gone, she would be well. The virtual-reality programs were designed around the same visualizations. Farrah stayed at the clinic for two weeks. I had a nearby hotel room. After the initial two-week visit, we came home. We returned to the clinic for three days every two weeks. It looked to me like she was getting better, but I didn't know if it was just my imagination. Dionicia told me my main job was to keep telling Farrah that the treatments were working and that she was looking stronger and stronger each day."

Mary took another sip of wine and continued. "You probably wondered why I hadn't invited you over to see Farrah over the past few months."

"We assumed she was getting too weak for visitors," Sheila said, "when we phoned, and you discouraged us from coming to visit. I must admit our feelings were a little hurt, but we didn't want to interfere."

"There is a very good reason I have kept her almost isolated. Dionicia told me that even well-meaning people could unintentionally undo most of our good progress if they inadvertently happened to make a remark to Farrah that caused her to doubt she was getting well. The smallest amount of doubt could be fatal to the treatment. Dionicia reminded me of the several instances in the Bible wherein Jesus cured people, telling them their faith had made them well, and then admonished them to go but tell no one about it. Jesus understood this faith principle perfectly. He realized the harmful effect that would result from the patient being subjected to negative input. I have been homeschooling Farrah throughout this process, carefully screening what she sees to make sure I don't introduce anything negative into her environment. The only music allowed in our house has been uplifting, joyful songs like the Beethoven piece she is playing upstairs. Dionicia told us inspiring music is an important part of creating a positive environment."

"When did you start to notice some improvement?"

"About a month after we started. It wasn't just my hopeful imagination. I took Farrah to Dr. Russell Colene for her regular monthly examination. Dr. Colene called me a week later when the test results came back. He told me it was very odd, but Farrah's blood cell count had improved a little. He said not to get too excited—it might be temporary or a defect with the lab's testing. I told him he was not to express any doubt in front of Farrah. I believed the tests would continue to show improvement. I told him to tell Farrah that he expected the improvement to continue. He agreed to never express any doubt in front of her.

"Sure enough, each following month, her tests came back more and more positive. For the last two months, there has been absolutely no sign that Farrah ever had the disease. It is gone, and we don't think it is coming back! You know I have always been a woman of faith. Almost every time the doors to the church are open, I am there. In spite of the tragedies that have befallen *mi familia*, I have always had a strong sense of spirituality. I believe we are physical, mental, and spiritual beings. I don't know why most of us don't tap into the spiritual essence of ourselves. It is the part that goes on forever, our divine nature, the part of us made in the image of God. Farrah's miracle has opened my eyes even wider. *Gracias a Dios!* Enough theology from this old woman tonight. We are all hungry. It smells like my sauce is ready. Sheila, if you'll help me, let's put the food on the table."

Mary called up the stairs for Farrah to join us.

Sheila and I stared, openmouthed, as the healthiest little girl you could ever hope to see bounded down the stairs, high-fived me, and gave Sheila a hug.

I don't think Sheila and I have ever enjoyed enchiladas as much as we enjoyed the ones that night. It was all we could do to keep our composure as we looked into the face of this bright little miracle child.

"Tia Sheila, why are you crying?" Farrah asked, looking concerned.

"I'm not crying, kiddo. I think your great-grandmother must have put too many onions on my enchilada."

As I sat quietly with Herb, so totally lost in thought, a single tear rolled down my cheek. The emotion of that scene with Mary and Farrah flooded back with enough power to really throw me.

"Anything wrong, Joe?" Herb asked, sounding concerned.

I took a deep breath and shook my head. "Far from it," I said. "Far from it!"

My eyes drifted around the room, almost as if I was seeing it for the first time. The walls of Herb's home were almost completely stacked with old books. Most of them were either reference books or classics. "How come you don't have any golf instruction books in your collection, Herb?" I queried.

"Never needed or wanted any," he replied. "Oh, I suppose there's nothing wrong with collecting golf books, just as long as you never read any of the damn things. One of the biggest problems for golfers is information overload. They receive too much conflicting information from instructors, books, magazines, and television. Makes them prone to jump from one method to the next instead of finding something simple that works and sticking with it. At the highest level, a golf swing is more about letting it happen than trying to make it happen. One of the main reasons you and I have been successful is that so far, we've managed to keep it simple and consistent. We want to keep it that way."

He paused, checking the date on his calendar. "Well, today was the shortest daylight day of the year. Each day will get longer now. Won't be all that long before we can move our practice sessions outside again."

Nodding in agreement, I swallowed the rest of my brandy and reluctantly rose from the comfortable chair. "Hate to go, but I better get on home, Herb. This combination of warm fire, comfortable chair, and apple brandy could turn anyone into a philosopher. I'm tempted to stay here and see if I start coming up with profound thoughts. Sheila has been really good about keeping supper warm for me, and she never questions the need for these evening sessions, but I don't want to push my luck. Don't get up," I said, bending down to shake his hand. "No use in waking Tootie again."

"Good night, and thanks for not keeping me awake, waiting for you to come up with something profound. That watched pot might never boil."

And sure enough, Herb was right. The watched pot didn't boil, but in reality it didn't need to because I was undergoing a long, voluntary indoctrination process. Herb called it brain handling, and when it all came down to it, I think he was right. I had to just *know* things would be different and believe that they actually would be. Herb and I worked hard on perfecting my golf moves throughout the winter. Slowly but surely, as predictable as the tides, the days grew longer, and the bitter winter winds of the Midwest diminished in their fury.

Toward the end of March, the moment of truth was near. The Masters Tournament in Augusta was just about on me. I must admit, Sheila and I were on pins and needles. I hadn't heard from God lately, and Sheila had stopped asking about Him. Of course, we both went to church. We said our prayers. We looked out for the less fortunate. But we stopped talking about the mission. We simply lived it. However, as date for the Masters drew closer, we both found ourselves strangely obsessed with looking for doves.

I was in my office to finish some pending loan presentations and reports at the end of March. Herb and I planned to leave for Augusta the next day, and I wanted to make sure my week out of the bank wouldn't be a major inconvenience for my customers and staff. In addition, a pile of unfinished work hanging over my head would be a major distraction during the tournament. It always amazed me how much work I could get done on a weekend without the distractions inherent to a typical business day. This Saturday was no exception. I breezed through most of the work stacked on my desk.

Herb and I had put in our final practice session the day before, followed by a scramble round in the afternoon. It was probably not appropriate to call it a scramble round, though, because I used only one ball. I shot a sixty-four. The months spent on my short game in Herb's barn and the mental focus developed through my morning meditations had improved my game beyond recognition. Once the weather got better, we had spent most of our time on the course rather than the practice range.

"Your technical skills are fine now," Herb told me. "We just need to keep fine-tuning your ability to take them to the course and shoot good scores."

After I dropped Herb at his place Friday night, Sheila and I went out for a nice dinner at her favorite restaurant. I wanted to thank her for her support and apologize for the amount of time I had spent away from home this past year. I felt guilty about taking off again, but at least this would be the last time. Our family budget didn't have room for two airline tickets and the other costs, such as hiring a dog-sitter, that would be associated with Sheila joining me. I knew she was disappointed, but I also knew Sheila was a practical woman. She understood budgets and limits. She understood me.

"Honey, I know this past year has been hard on you. Please understand I never would have put you through all this if it weren't about much more than just playing in a golf tournament. In many ways, your encouragement and support have been even more important than Herb's," I said.

I held her hands in mine. I leaned close. Her scent was comforting and arousing in a sedate sort of way. I knew then that I'd never loved anyone more. Sheila looked at me, tears welling up in her eyes. My compliment had caught her a little off-guard, I guess—probably because, like most husbands, I didn't compliment my wife nearly often enough.

Shaking her head slightly, she replied, "I have to admit that I had my doubts. It all seems so implausible. It wasn't until you won the club championship that I really believed you could do this. I couldn't be more thrilled and proud about what you are doing. Herb and I have telephone conversations almost every day. He keeps reminding me not to inject any doubt into your 'banker brain.' I really enjoyed taking care of Tootie while you both were at the Mid-Amateur. Herb asked me to watch her again next week. It will be fun. She is great company. We like the same soap operas on TV."

The rest of our evening was incredible.

Jolted from my reverie, I set about finishing the last of the reports I was working on. Just then, I heard a ding from my computer. I swiveled around and smiled at the chat window that had just opened on my screen. It was like an old friend was dropping by unexpectedly. Although the messages from God had never been threatening, my hands were shaking. I still found it a little disconcerting to be in direct communication with the Creator of the universe.

> *"Good afternoon, Joe! Just wanted to tell you I'm very pleased with the work you and Herb have done and ask if you have any questions before you leave for Augusta."*

"As a matter of fact, I do," I responded, typing rapidly. "One occurred to me this morning as I was driving to the office. If I win the tournament and become this shining example of how much more capable people are than they realize, won't I be asked a whole lot of questions? Folks are liable to get it into their heads that I am some sort of a guru with lots of answers. Don't you need to make me smarter? I'll be like a twenty-watt bulb trying to do the sun's job."

> *"Make an old banker smarter? It would be easier to part the Red Sea again! Win one golf tournament, and now you're going to be a prophet? Ready and able to explain the mysteries of the universe? Maybe we should revise the Bible, so we can add the Book of Joe.*
>
> *"Relax. I'm just giving you a hard time—one of the perks that go along with being God. Don't worry. I*

am not expecting more than you can deliver. You don't need to overthink this. Your mission is no more than what we talked about a year ago. Just use the victory as a platform to tell people about eliminating their self-imposed limitations. Tell them to set great goals for themselves. Tell them about creating more time by changing their concept of a day. Tell them to take me on as their partner.

"Most people would jump at the opportunity to go into business with the world's greatest businessman or cowrite a novel with the world's greatest author. Their success would be assured. Yet they don't take advantage of my availability and willingness to help them with any worthy endeavor. I am always there, and I am always available. If people would realize how omnipresent and approachable I am, most of the world's problems wouldn't exist."

"I'm glad you don't expect me to be some sort of prophet, but it seems only natural for people to assume I know a lot more than I actually do."

"You will be given answers as you need them. Let's give it a try. Ask me a question—something you can't explain."

I read and reread God's message. It struck me that I really must be insane to believe all this. But I'd bought the whole thing—hook, line, and sinker—and I wanted it to continue. I also wanted to win the Masters. I began typing again.

I wrote, "When it comes to things I can't explain, you're talking about a rather large range. It is probably infinitely larger than the range of things I *can* explain. Okay, how about evolution? Lots of people cite evolution as proof that you don't exist. So how about that? What do you have to say about Darwin and his ideas?"

"Of course there is evolution. The evidence is everywhere. This wonderful process has always been part of my plan. My design calls for a continuous process of refinement and improvement. This is probably going to shock you, but I am also continuing to evolve. I find it to be very enjoyable. Why would I deny myself this experience? I have been around forever, literally billions of years. It would be extremely boring for me if I weren't constantly evolving."

"Whoa there! *You* are evolving? I have always been told that you are perfect and unchanging!"

"Easy to get hung up on semantics here. Depends on your definition of 'perfect.' My definition of perfection excludes stagnation. By my definition, I am perfect. The unchanging aspect of me is my love for my creation, of which you are a part. What continues to change is the way I demonstrate my love, in response to the evolving nature of my creation. Evolution is a fact. You do not have a choice about whether or not you will continue to evolve, but you do have a considerable amount of choice about how you will evolve. Animals don't have much choice. A cow today knows nothing more than a cow did in biblical times. Consider how far humans have advanced over the same time period."

"Some might argue that evolution is simply nature's way of correcting mistakes, and if indeed mistakes were made, no perfect god made this universe. Did you ever make any mistakes?"

"It has been mentioned that I made the pit in the avocado too big. And I suppose if I had to do it again, I would add one more commandment: something on the order of

'Thou shalt establish short and strict term limits upon thy politicians.' Sorry, Joe—can't resist a little levity at times. Actually, I can resist it; I just choose not to. Sometimes I think it was a mistake not to give humans a better sense of humor. Please recognize I am using the term 'mistake' only to stay within a context that you can understand. I don't make mistakes, although something can appear to be a mistake from the human perspective. Often what humans call a mistake is really a blessing in disguise. How's that for an answer?"

"Perfect, from what I can tell, though above what my little twenty-watt bulb can handle. I'm feeling better. It is a huge relief to know you will be giving me answers as I need them, as well as the ability to defer, when necessary. Thanks for this conversation. I think I'm clear again. I don't have to worry about anything beyond the scope of what you assigned to me last April. You'll take care of the rest."

"Bingo! I use that expletive a lot around Catholics. Don't worry. Just keep trusting me and listening to Herb. By the way, this is the last time I will communicate with you through e-mail."

"I just knew you would want to revert back to stone tablets sooner or later!"

"Very funny. I have constantly communicated with you since the day you were born. Like most humans, you believe our communication has been a monologue, with you doing all the talking, since I don't prefer to respond with words. Words have too many limitations. My answers most often come in a different form: a gut feeling on your part, a chance encounter with a friend, a song on the radio, an occurrence you misinterpret as a

87

coincidence. I will never stop answering you. Just learn to listen. We will do just fine.

"One more piece of advice. I have kept our communication rather light and humorous, even though I am very serious about your mission. Many people do not see me this way. It has always been my desire to make each of you unique. No two of you are alike. I relate to each of you in a manner that works best for the way I created you. Some of you are best served by seeing me as stern and demanding, others by seeing me as a loving grandfatherly figure. There are infinite combinations and variations, unique to each of you. I gave Joe Goodman a strong sense of humor. Therefore, I have used humor as an important part of our communication. It will be natural for you to use humor as you communicate the message from our mission. However, be careful. Many people will accept it better if you use less humor than your natural inclination.

"Now go home and get some rest."

This latest exchange with God left me wanting even more. God's funny like that. Once you get into it with Him, you're going to be intrigued. You'll find you have so many questions that it's impossible to get all the answers, and that's okay. I don't think we're even supposed to have all the answers anyway, even if we think we want to have them.

I was smiling as I left the office on that late Saturday afternoon. For a short while, I didn't think about work or the upcoming tourney in Augusta. When I arrived home, Sheila met me at the door with a warm hug, a kiss on the cheek, and a nice pot roast she'd made in the slow cooker.

Later, just before we went to sleep, she kissed me good night. "You know," she whispered, "you're a very special man."

Holding her close, I said, "Aw, shucks, you don't really mean it, do you?"

She laughed. "Aw, shucks yourself, you big oaf!"

"Who're you callin' a big oaf?"

"You!"

"Thanks a lot! Like that's supposed to help me beat the pants off the young tykes in Augusta."

We were silent for a long moment.

"Seriously, Joe," she said, "you're special, and don't you forget it. You're the most special man in the whole world!"

I suddenly felt tears in my eyes. I swallowed hard. "Honey, no matter what happens, you know that I love you, right?"

She reached over and squeezed my hand. "I know, my love. Now you get some sleep. You've got a long day tomorrow with Herb."

"Herb. Yeah, Herb."

"Yeah," she said, yawning, "Herb."

Herb arrived at my house early Sunday morning to drop off Tootie. We planned to take my car to the airport and leave it in long-term parking for the week. As she walked through the front door, Tootie was wagging her tail enthusiastically, no doubt anticipating being spoiled rotten again by Sheila in our absence.

I hugged Sheila, wishing she could go along. "Honey," she said, tears welling up in her eyes, "I remember a few years ago listening to an interview with a golfer who had just blown a big lead in a tournament. He remarked that even though he hadn't won, his dog and his wife would still love him. I can't speak for Tootie, but I promise I will be here for you, win or lose. I am incredibly proud of how far you've come. God picked the right two guys for this mission."

Starting to choke up, I kissed her again and edged toward the door, giving Tootie a good-bye pat on the head. The dog appeared rather noncommittal about her future loyalty in the event I failed. Sheila stood by the door and waved as we took off.

Herb being Herb, we used most of the time en route to the airport and on the flight visualizing what we were likely to encounter at Augusta.

"Now that we are actually on our way, it seems so surreal, Herb," I whispered as he sat next to me in economy class. I was filled with a mixture of anticipation and dread. Here I was, an aging banker, about to compete on the biggest stage in golf, armed only with a faith that I wasn't sure was unshakable. Herb didn't say anything; he just patted my knee as he stared out of the window. I hoped he was feeling more confident than I was. He had to be my rock.

CHAPTER 8

WHEN OUR PLANE TOUCHED DOWN, WE WERE SWEPT UP IN THE moment. We checked into the nicest hotel I could afford. We had a bite to eat, though I wasn't hungry. I noticed that Herb was unusually silent. For once, words seemed to escape him. I wasn't sure whether that was a good thing or a bad thing. In fact, I found it rather unsettling. I said nothing about it. I was too on edge.

The entire experience was a whirlwind. Looking back on it now, I can hardly remember the little details, the crowds, or the other golfers. But I do recall that as Herb and I trekked toward the first tee to get set for my opening drive, he began to banter with me. In the olden days, a caddy just carried clubs. Nowadays, especially in professional golf, the caddy holds a much expanded role. Often your best friend, he or she serves as coach and motivator. I was counting on Herb, who I firmly believed was acting as God's conduit.

Everything was a blur for the first three rounds. Our routine of intense focus during the shot-making process, coupled with complete distraction between shots, had served us very well, just as it had during the club championship and the Mid-Amateur tournament. We managed to shoot even-par seventy-twos each of the first three trips around the course. Our strategy, for the most part, had been to play approach shots to the middle of the greens and try to two-putt. Given the speed and complexity of the greens at Augusta National, most Masters pundits would think it foolhardy to depend on two-putting from thirty or forty feet every hole. However, none of these pundits

Joe S. Bullock

were recent graduates of Herb's "distance control for fast greens" training program. The floor of Herb's barn was smooth concrete. For hour upon hour over the winter, Herb had had me hitting long lag putts to steering wheel–sized circles on this floor, not letting me quit until I could lag three out of four within the circle from varying distances up to sixty feet. If you could do that on concrete, even Augusta's greens didn't seem intimidatingly fast.

"What's your favorite line from any movie you've seen, Joe?" Herb inquired as we trekked down the first fairway. I was relieved that we had managed to start the fourth and final round with a respectable tee shot, which had required that I maintain maximum focus, to avoid being overwhelmed by the circumstances. Once again, Herb was now decompressing me. He knew responding to the question would require the right amount of thought to snap me out of my shot focus.

"Heck, Herb, never really thought about it. I guess an obvious answer would be something like *Gone with the Wind*'s 'Frankly, Scarlett, I don't give a damn,' or Clint Eastwood's classic, 'Go ahead, make my day.' Oh, wait! I know! My favorite line is from that Jack Nicholson movie *As Good As It Gets*. 'You make me want to be a better man.' I use it all the time when Sheila gets mad at me. It almost always makes her smile and forgive me. What's yours?"

"Easy. First *Jaws* movie. Sheriff Brody is chumming off the end of the boat when he gets his first close-up glimpse of the shark. He turns around, about to mess his britches, and says, 'You're going to need a bigger boat!' Love the line for a couple of reasons. First of all, boy, was he right! Second, it applies so much to all of us. We all need bigger boats. We have to build them for ourselves. Bigger confidence, bigger trust, bigger faith."

My ball was sitting up nicely on the perfectly mowed grass. The diminutive drive had barely reached the first portion of the dogleg, allowing a sight line at only the left edge of the green. My approach shot would have to be a fade. "Time to turn the focus back on, kid," Herb advised. "Distance to the pin, cut back right, is 203 yards. Middle of the green is 190. We need to carry just over the front, which is 180.

92

Let's hit the Slice Hotch at full choke. Should carry to the front and run into the middle."

I focused on the shot and executed a good swing, producing a shot that reasonably resembled our plan. The ball finished near the middle of the green, about thirty-five feet from the cup. My effort drew very little applause from the gallery behind the green—another yawner as far as they were concerned. My playing partner, Billy Dale Rankin, used what appeared to be a nine-iron to hit his ball to six feet. This shot drew substantially more applause. He tipped his visor and strode confidently toward the green, smelling an easy birdie.

"That Nicholson movie had a couple of other good lines, as I recall." Herb stated, bringing me out of the shot. "Remember when he dumped the little dog down the laundry chute?"

"Oh yeah," I replied, seeing the scene in my mind. "Not sure Tootie would appreciate getting tossed down the chute and being told, 'This is New York: if you can make it here, you can make it anywhere!' Let's not let Tootie know we thought it was funny." We chuckled all the way to the green. I marked my ball and began reading the putt. Herb agreed with me, gauging that the putt was slightly uphill and would turn a couple of feet to the right. I went through my routine and stroked it smoothly. The ball coasted to a stop six inches from the cup. I walked up and tapped it in for a no-sweat par.

Billy Dale didn't consult with his caddy. He took one look at the hole and hit the ball firmly—a bit too firmly. It caught the edge on the high side and spun out, trickling away a good three feet. A little unnerved, he pushed the three-footer wide of the cup, turning what had appeared to be a cinch birdie into an ugly bogey. You could have fried an egg on his forehead as we strode to the second tee. His caddy, Wiley Weaver, was an old hand. Word had it that Rankin's parents had insisted he hire the most experienced caddy available to help him acclimate to life on the tour. Although he had won the NCAA individual title, as well as several big amateur tournaments, the tour was a whole different environment.

Wiley was saying all the right things to calm his man down. What he probably wanted to say was something on the order of "if you had taken the time to consult with me, young man, I would have told you that putt was faster than it looked." I guess that's what he would have said, anyway, and I guess Wiley probably knew enough to bite his tongue. I know I would have were I in his shoes.

Walking over to the second tee, Herb muttered out of the side of his mouth, "That boy is going to have a tough time today. He's under a lot of perceived pressure, trying to live up to all the potential everyone says he has."

"That's one of the few good things about being my age," I whispered. "By the time you turn sixty, people quit talking about your potential. If you had any, they realize it probably would have shown up by now."

Herb laughed and then quickly covered his mouth to conceal the grin created by my little nugget of wisdom. "Good point," he said.

Herb didn't want Billy Dale or Wiley to think he was grinning about the missed putt. I was sort of proud of myself. It wasn't very often I came up with something Herb thought was clever, though I'd been doing it more often of late.

The second hole was a downhill par five, sweeping from right to left. Most of the field could easily get home in two if they successfully shaped their drives between the bunker on the right and the trees along the left edge. Since I couldn't reach the bunker, the fairway played wider for me. I went through my preshot routine, aimed at the bunker, and hit a slight draw, which ended up in the middle of the fairway.

Billy Dale teed his ball and took a couple of vicious practice swings, no doubt intent on smashing his ball within middle-iron distance for his second shot. If he could walk away with an eagle, this would more than make up for his foolish bogey on the first. He rushed his backswing and ripped at the ball. Not surprisingly, his herculean effort resulted in his coming over the top as he started his downswing, creating a snap hook that propelled his ball deep into the left-side trees. He slammed his driver into the ground and strode angrily off the tee box.

"He needs to slow down and listen to Wiley," Herb said to me as we walked toward my ball. "Didn't need anything more than his average drive to get into position to hit the green for an eagle putt. Pressing for a few more yards didn't make sense."

We talked about how Billy Dale's experience this week had been so different from mine. He had arrived Monday with his entourage of agents and assistants, all of whom had been invited to share the home of a wealthy club member for the week, whereas Herb and I were staying at a cut-rate motel thirty minutes from the course. Upon arriving at the practice range, he had been surrounded by fans wanting his autograph. Nobody had paid any attention to us. Veteran pros as well as media members had stopped by the practice tee to observe as he put on an amazing ball-striking display. A couple of past champions had offered to play practice rounds with him, volunteering to impart course knowledge gained through decades of playing in the tournament.

Through it all, I had gone pretty much unnoticed. Not exactly a household name, I'd had to show my player's badge to the security guard to be allowed on the premises. None of the other players had approached me. I understood. I was sort of a pariah. Never had a player who'd qualified for the Masters by way of winning the Mid-Amateur survived the thirty-six-hole cut. No one had invited me to join them for a practice round. It was as if the other contestants believed bad golf was contagious, and they couldn't risk exposure to me just prior to a major tournament. The only attention I received was on the practice range Monday morning. A smart-ass young swing coach paused to watch me hit balls. He had contracted to coach several of the players in the tournament and was apparently killing time while waiting for one of them to show up on the range. As he watched me hit balls, his face took on the expression of someone observing the runt of a litter of puppies, speculating that the little dog would not last long. I hit several old-guy shots with my driver and turned around. "Any suggestions?" I asked, trying to be friendly.

"Hey, pal, I specialize in swing changes. What you need is a complete body change," he smirked, loud enough so that most of the spectators behind the range could hear him. I had to admit, I thought it was pretty funny. The guy heard a low growl coming from Herb and beat a hasty retreat.

As we arrived at my ball, Herb reminded me to refocus. He handed me the Hook Hotch, advising, "Choke this down all the way and hit a little draw down the middle. It should end up slightly to the left, taking that nasty bunker a little more out of play. At full choke you should leave yourself back far enough to be able to put some spin on your third shot."

I went through my routine and hit a respectable little lay-up shot safely to the left-center of the fairway. After handing the Hook Hotch to Herb, I turned to see what appeared to be a rather heated debate between Billy Dale and Wiley Weaver. Wiley was trying to convince his man to safely punch the ball back into the fairway. From there he could hit a long iron to the green, giving him a good chance to escape with par. Billy Dale was having none of it. He had spied a small opening in the trees ahead and was determined to get back the stroke he'd lost at the first hole. Shrugging in resignation, Wiley put the pitching wedge back in the bag and handed Billy Dale a long iron. Carefully aiming at the small gap between two giant pines, the young man took a powerful swing, producing a stinging line drive. He almost pulled it off. At the last moment, the ball struck the underside of a limb. It dropped straight down, nestling against an exposed root. Billy Dale stomped up to the ball. It was clearly unplayable. His fight temporarily gone, he meekly took his drop, accepted the pitching wedge from Wiley, and punched out to the fairway, two strokes worse off than if he had taken his caddy's advice.

After watching my playing companion hit his fifth shot into the greenside bunker, Herb and I continued down the fairway. "This reminds me of a lesson I learned in college," I told Herb. "The best player on our team was a guy named Van Austin. He was a small-town guy like me, but he could really play. I remember asking him one time why he was able to score better than the rest of us. He told me it was because he could smell a double-bogey coming, and he didn't let it happen. If he got in trouble, he figured out how he could limit the damage to a bogey, rather than trying to be a hero. He almost always made several birdies in a round, so a couple of bogies didn't ruin his score."

Herb judged my third shot to be eighty-seven yards. Consulting my wedge chart, we determined I could use either a full-lob wedge or a three-quarter sand wedge. Even from this angle, it was a bit of a sucker pin. Herb picked out a point to aim at thirty feet left of the hole. "Don't you think we should start being a little more aggressive?" I asked. "We started out four strokes behind, and it doesn't look like even par is going to win this thing."

"Too early in the round to make our move," Herb countered. "A mistake at this point could be fatal. Let's stick with our conservative strategy for now. Hit the sand wedge, taking a little off it. I never like to see anyone go after a lob wedge hard."

I went into my routine, but my focus wasn't strong. I doubted our strategy and was afraid I would hit the sand wedge too far. As a result, I decelerated into the ball and hit the shot slightly fat. Luckily, the ball landed three yards short of the putting surface and took a fortuitous bounce up on the front of the green, leaving me with a putt not much more difficult than I would have had if I'd hit the shot correctly.

Herb knew exactly what had happened. "You weren't confident. As a result, you lost your focus," he admonished. "Bound to happen now and then. You're only human. We got away with it this time, but you will need to be a lot sharper as the round goes on. The back nine will be very nerve-racking if your focus isn't superstrong."

Billy Dale blasted out of the trap to six feet and two-putted for a triple bogey. He had started the round at one under par, a stroke ahead of me and three strokes behind the coleaders. After going four over for the first two holes, he was now well off the pace.

Herb and I got a good read on my putt, and I almost holed it. My ball lipped out and stopped on the edge, for a tap-in par.

"That was almost an unexpected bonus," I remarked as we walked off the green. "When the ball was about two inches from the cup, I was sure it was going in."

"Would have been nice," Herb agreed. "But I am darn tickled with our even-par start. Young Mr. Rankin would surely love to have those two pars on his card. Maybe he will learn to let Wiley help him. It doesn't do much good to have an experienced guy on your bag if you won't listen to him."

"Even if the experienced guy is a somewhat sanctimonious old fart?"

"Especially if the experienced guy is a somewhat sanctimonious old fart," Herb replied, grinning all the way to the third tee.

Arriving at the third tee, we discovered we would have a delay. The group ahead of us was still standing by their drives, waiting for the twosome ahead of them to clear the green. One of the players on the green had called for a rules official. His ball had inadvertently moved while he was addressing it, invoking one of those silly little rulings that make the game so delightfully maddening. The rules official was just now arriving on the scene.

Herb and I were standing on the far side of the tee, out of earshot from anyone.

"Herb," I asked, "what if I need some more help? In view of what just happened with that wedge shot, would it be all right if I prayed for more confidence and better focus? Seems like it might be selfish to pray for help to beat these other guys. They aren't bad people."

"Couldn't hurt a bit," Herb replied. "First of all, this doesn't have anything to do with whether these other golfers are good people. I bet they are great people, but it would hardly cause a ripple outside of the golf world if one of them won. Have faith that the greater worldwide good would be for you to win and then deliver your message. Remember, you are here because God picked you for this mission. He gave you all the tools you need. You need to provide the faith.

"Second, it is never selfish to pray for God to help you do something that is righteous. Most folks have a limited view of God. They fail to realize He is both universal and very personal. He can listen and respond to a prayer from an individual such as you without diluting His ability to do the same for countless billions of other people at the same time. He is the ultimate multitasker.

"Therefore, it is not selfish to pray because you are not asking God to give your prayer priority over other prayers, either in chronological urgency or in critical importance. He doesn't have to prioritize. He is constantly responding appropriately to every heartfelt prayer. When people don't think there has been a response, it's only because they don't recognize what the appropriate response was. It very often isn't the anticipated response."

"That's pretty deep for me, Herb," I responded. "Need to chew on it for a while. I feel better, just listening to what you said, even though I don't think I fully grasp it."

"Just go on faith, grasshopper," Herb reassured me, crudely imitating a Zen master. "A lot of this involves the ability to know without understanding, or at least without being able to verbalize it. Remember back to one of our first conversations. What you are being dictates what you are feeling. Just try being relaxed, confident, and focused, sort of like you are an actor who is playing the role of a relaxed, confident, focused guy. If you can do this, you will feel relaxed, confident, and focused, which will be reflected in your shot execution."

As we waited for the fairway to clear, Herb and I discussed our strategy. We decided to stick with the way we had played the hole the first three rounds. The third hole was the shortest par four at Augusta. Most of the field would wrestle with a decision of whether to attack aggressively with a driver, leaving a very short second shot but risking trouble, or lay back short of the bunkers along the left side of the fairway. The bunkers were located at a distance within reach of my driver. We decided to go with the Slice Hotch, aim down the left side, and cut the ball toward the middle. Bolstered by Herb's assurance, I whispered a little prayer, settled into my routine, and hit a very respectable shot, almost exactly as we had planned.

Wiley Weaver made a move to stop the bleeding. A no-sweat par would go a long way to settle his young player's nerves. He pulled a four-iron from the bag. To my surprise, Rankin nodded in agreement and hit his ball about ten feet to the right of my tee shot.

"Time to lighten this back up," Herb stated as we climbed the fairway. "Consider this. Columbus named this place America, after his good friend Americus Vespucci. What if his good friend had been named Murray? Would we now be living in the United States of Murray?"

"Maybe," I replied. "Can't you just hear Kate Smith's rousing rendition of 'God Bless Murray'?"

After a few stupid attempts at singing the song with our revised lyrics, we arrived at my ball, feeling loose and relaxed. I had 120 yards to a pin cut in the back middle. I went into my routine and hit a nine-iron about twenty feet below the hole. Billy Dale hit his gap wedge, finishing pin high, fifteen feet left of the hole.

We two-putted for pars and headed for the fourth tee.

The fourth hole at Augusta was an intimidating 240-yard par three. It played downhill, magnifying the effect of any wind. The front was guarded by a large, scary bunker on the right. It was extremely difficult for a golfer to get up and down for par from this bunker because the green slopes severely away from the right.

The group ahead had holed out quickly and left the green as we arrived on the tee. Herb sat the bag down and grabbed a small amount of grass, tossing it in the air. "Looks like we're hitting into a little headwind today," he observed. "Kind of wish we weren't hitting first. It's going to be tough to judge the distance. Can't risk hitting it into the bunker, so if we're wrong, let's err on the long side. Go with the Hook Hotch unchoked, aiming over the center of the bunker. It'll probably go to the back of the green. We'll have to figure out how to two-putt from there. Heck of a lot better than messing with that trap."

"Sounds like a plan, boss," I replied. "I don't want any part of that bunker. Ball would be coming down so steeply from up here, it would almost have to plug. Might take me a week to get it out of there."

I stepped forward and took my shot. Good focus, good swing, good shot, slightly too much club. My ball landed well past the pin and came to rest about six feet from the back edge of the green.

Wiley gave Herb a look of mock disgust. "Most of the time I can get a good idea of what club to pull by watching the first guy hit," he lamented. "But how the hell can I club off that contraption? Might as well use a Ouija Board." The four of us got a good laugh out of Wiley's remark. For the first time Billy Dale appeared to be relaxing a little. He took the four-iron Wiley handed him and hit a superb shot, a low line drive that penetrated the wind, rising at the end and landing gently ten feet below the cup.

Walking down the slope to the green, Herb whispered, "How about that shot the kid just hit? I bet there's not five other players in the field who could hit a shot like that. He has as much physical talent and technical ability as anybody in the world. If he would change his concept of a day and use the time in the morning to focus on his mental game and spiritual strength, he could become just about unbeatable."

"I agree. I wish I had changed my concept of what a day is back when I was his age. It's depressing to think about how many opportunities I let slip by while I was lying in bed every morning."

Herb and I surveyed my lengthy birdie putt. "Pretty obvious break to read," Herb observed. "Speed is going to be the challenge. Just take a few practice strokes and completely trust your sense of feel. Focus on being smooth."

I hit a darn good putt, considering the length and downslope. The ball finished four feet below the hole. I marked my ball and watched as Billy Dale holed his birdie putt. Staying focused and in the moment, I replaced my ball and body-putted it into the back of the hole. The ability to focus better, along with the simple method Herb had taught me, had taken my short putting from a weakness to a strength. Golf is a lot more enjoyable when you aren't sweating blood over the short putts.

We arrived at the fifth tee and found the fairway wide open. The group ahead had already played their approach shots and moved out of range. The fifth hole was one of the tougher par fours at Augusta. It played 455 yards, to a very difficult green. The tee shot was uphill to a tight landing area between two hungry bunkers on the left and a forest on the right. Billy Dale's impressive birdie on four gave him the honors. Bolstered by his performance on the last two holes, he hit a massive draw down the right rough line, curving perfectly into the fairway. Once again, my lack of length created a wider target for me since I couldn't reach the bunkers. I hit a very long drive by my modest standards. The ball started down the middle, kicked off the slope, and finished in the fairway just short of the first bunker on the left.

"That was a good poke for you. Very un-geezer-like," Herb said as we trudged up the slope. "Thought for a second you hit it hard enough to reach that bunker."

"Yeah, if I would have swung any harder, I probably would have hurt myself. Don't know what got into me. I guess I saw how far the kid just hit it, and it spurred something inside me. Pretty foolish. The only thing the extra effort did was almost bring the bunker into play."

My lie was a little awkward, the ball above my feet on the side slope. Herb and I considered our options for the approach shot. The last thing we wanted was to hit the shot too long. A long approach would either catch the rear bunker or go down a steep slope into an impossible lie. The pin was cut in the back, tempting a golfer to take the risk.

Herb was thinking out loud, creating our strategy as he spoke. "We could hit the Slice Hotch to offset the stance, but to get anywhere close, we would have to carry it well up on the green. A fade is going to sit down pretty quickly. If we went with the Hook Hotch, we could land it well short and let it run to the middle. Seems like a smarter play to me. If we misjudge it, we have a fairly good chance of getting up and down from the front. Almost no chance if we go long."

I nodded in agreement. This was going to be tough. I recalled that God had said there were no guarantees in games or in life. Doubt flooded me. If only I knew winning was a sure thing, then I could relax and enjoy the ride. But the win wasn't in the bag. It never was and never would be. This was just something I knew I had to try for, not for me or even for Herb, but for the bigger issues in play. I felt a little better when I took the Hook Hotch from Herb. I choked it to the quarter-choke mark and made a much smoother swing than I had on my tee shot. The ball landed about five feet on the front of the green and rolled out to twenty-five feet below the hole.

"Just what the doctor ordered!" Herb said with a grin. "Fairly easy two-putt from there. Four is always a good score on this hole."

I looked over and saw Billy Dale and Wiley considering their approach options. His booming drive left only 145 yards to the pin. I could clearly hear them debating whether the approach was a nine-iron or a hard pitching wedge. A nine-iron shot would reach the pin but would bring all the trouble behind the green into play. They decided to take the risk and go with the nine. After the poor start, they needed to make something happen in order to get back into contention. Billy Dale made a good swing, sending the ball in a towering arc, on a perfect line at the pin. The ball landed twelve feet above the hole and inexplicably didn't spin back, remaining just inches from the ball mark. I saw Wiley grimace, knowing how tricky the putt was from above the hole.

"That's a tough break," Herb mused. "You'd expect a ball flown to that spot would spin back down by the hole. He did everything right and wasn't rewarded. Watch him shaking his head as he marches to the green. He needs to make an important choice, and he needs to make it in a hurry. He can choose to let this bad break bother him, or he can choose to accept it as part of the challenge and concentrate on making a good stroke on this putt."

I shook my head and glanced over at Herb. "You're going all profound on me now? Really?"

"No time like the present," he said.

"What you just said could be said about life, you know."

Herb said nothing. He just shot me the most conspiratorial look I've ever seen to this day. Then Herb said, "Instead of feeling sorry for himself, he should be thinking something on the order of 'This gives me a chance to show what a great putter I am.'"

That was one of the great things about golf, I thought. The game so often mirrored real life. Playing golf was a good way to learn some of life's harder lessons in a relatively bloodless arena. I'd known this for a long time, of course, but playing golf under Herb's instruction had brought the notion home.

"You mean like how to turn lemons into lemonade?" I offered.

"Exactly," Herb responded, grinning at me as I marked my ball.

"You remind me of my dad. He once told me the smartest thing he'd ever learned was about making choices. Dad said you rarely have complete control over what happens to you in life, but you almost always have complete control over how you choose to respond."

As we proceeded down the course, Herb said, "Smart man."

"Yeah," I said, "smart man. He also told me not to look for unfairness because I would always find it. Life was never intended to be fair. Dwelling on unfairness detracts from the joy of life because it leads to being unhappy and bitter. We are better served by accepting unfairness as just one of the challenges that make us stronger. Hmm, I just had a strange thought. Do you think God is trying to help me by giving Billy Dale a bad break, or is He multitasking again, trying to teach Billy Dale lessons as we go along?"

"If I had to pick," Herb said, "I'd say it was the second option. Remember, this is a testimony of the power of faith, and that wouldn't be the case if God was helping you by wreaking havoc with the other players."

We studied my putt. It was decidedly uphill. "There are not many truly slow putts at Augusta," Herb advised, "but this one is about like you were in college math classes: pretty darn slow."

"Main reason I didn't major in engineering," I responded, feigning indignation. "Instead, I went into banking! No math involved there!"

"Very funny."

"Not meant to be," I said, suppressing a laugh.

"Okay, wise guy, just hit this putt a little harder than it looks like you have to." Herb chuckled. "Look at a spot about three feet above the hole, and pretend that's where the hole is."

I gave the ball a healthy rap. At first, it looked as if I had hit it too hard, but the ball quickly ran out of enthusiasm for fighting gravity. It finished a foot short of the hole, leaving an easy tap-in.

Based on my casual observations, it looked as though Wiley had managed to help Billy Dale shake off his disappointment and concentrate on his lightning-fast putt. He made a great effort, judging the speed and the break almost perfectly. At the last roll, the ball turned sharply, caught the bottom lip, and stopped less than an inch from the cup. Even though the putt didn't go in, it was a small victory. After two almost perfect shots, it would have been easy for the young man to be overly aggressive on the putt, thinking the hole owed him a birdie. An aggressive first putt could have easily led to a three-putt bogey.

I poked Herb in the shoulder. "Hey, looks like the guy's got his game back," I said.

Herb looked worried. "Yes, it does," he said.

CHAPTER 9

||||||||||||||||||||||||||||||||||||||||||||||||||||||||||||||||||||||||||||||||||||||||||||||||||||||||||||||||||||||||||||

WE EXITED THE FIFTH GREEN THROUGH THE GALLERY ROPES ON the left side and made our way to the sixth tee.

"Haven't heard any roars from the gallery for the group behind us," Herb noted. "Let's check out the scoreboard behind the tee and see what's going on."

The scoreboard revealed the leaders were struggling. Playing in the final pairing on Sunday at Augusta could unnerve even the most experienced players. Both Scott Thomas and Michael Cameron were seasoned touring pros with multiple wins, including two majors apiece. Neither had birdied the second hole, although each had the length to easily reach it in two shots. Equally shocking, both had bogeyed the fourth, Thomas from the front bunker and Cameron with a three putt from the back edge.

Herb knew how distracting it was for me to find out I was now only three shots out of the lead. "Lots of golf left. Play your own game. Play one shot at a time. Don't worry about what the other guys are doing," Herb rattled off. "If I can think of any more clichés, I'll throw them in as well. How about make sure you've got on clean underwear in case you get into an accident?"

"I don't know about getting into an accident," I replied. "But having an underwear-related incident is certainly a distinct possibility. This is way outside of my comfort zone."

I glanced over at Herb, hoping to see his comforting smile. He wasn't smiling, but he was looking at me with a gleam in his eye.

I could sense that he was in the hunt, like a hound closing in on a petrified fox.

"Just keep playing the role of a relaxed, confident, focused guy," Herb assured me. "If you can do that and maintain your faith in the outcome, we will be just fine."

Maintaining the honor following his par on the previous hole, Billy Dale prepared to hit first. The sixth hole was a sharply downhill 180-yard par three. The pin was set in the usual Sunday position, on a small shelf in the back right portion. Although this took the large front bunker out of play, it presented a very challenging target. If you missed on the right, you were short-sided, with the green sloping sharply away. A shot landing left of the small shelf would trickle far down the slope, leaving an extremely difficult two-putt.

Billy Dale hit a very respectable shot, landing on the small shelf and rolling just off the green, pin high.

"That is one tough pin," Herb observed, stroking his chin. "Always is on Sunday. I like a six-iron, aimed at the middle, with a little cut on it. The fat guy wearing the red shirt in the gallery behind the green would be a good starting line."

"You always told me to pick a precise, small target, Herb. That guy is anything but small. Shouldn't we pick a skinny guy or a small child for a target?" I asked with mock concern.

I could see that Herb loved my response. Maintaining my sense of humor would be crucial to staying relaxed. "Nah, always go with a fat guy. They move around less than your other choices. No sense trying to hit a moving target."

Still smiling, I made a decent swing and hit a shot to thirty feet left of the hole. Not the bravest of efforts, but a good chance for a two-putt par. I was beginning to think I might actually have a shot at winning this thing, but I told myself not to get ahead of myself.

Just do your best, I thought. *Let God take care of the rest!*

When we arrived at the green, Herb admonished me once again to hit my putt a little harder than my first instinct would suggest. If I left it short of the shelf, it could very well roll back at me. Picking a spot behind the hole as a target, I gave it a firm effort and was pleased to see the ball stop within easy tap-in distance.

Billy Dale's ball was resting in a good lie, just over twenty feet from the cup. He had a good chance to hole it from this position and almost did. The ball slid by on the right edge and wandered three feet past. He took his time on the come-back putt and hit it squarely in the middle.

Given the difficult pin position, I'm sure he was as happy as I was to walk off the green with a par.

Herb and I arrived on the seventh tee feeling very satisfied with our opening string of six pars. Boring golf was usually very effective in the last round of a major.

The seventh hole was one of the tightest driving holes on the course. It had been lengthened a few years earlier to 450 yards in order to force the longer hitters to hit their driver or three-wood from the tee, to have a short-iron approach. Before the tee had been moved back, most of the long-hitting field would use hybrids or long irons off the tee, to increase their odds of staying in the fairway. The green here was one of the smallest at Augusta and very well-bunkered. The approach shot was difficult, even from short-iron distance. The hole had given me trouble all week. I had to hit a driver to have any chance of reaching the green in regulation. My best effort off the tee had left me with a second shot of around two hundred yards to the very difficult target. I had scored two bogies and a par in the first three rounds.

After watching my playing companion hit another tremendous drive into the middle of the fairway, I teed my ball on the left side of the tee box, intending to hit a draw. I was trying to finish on the flat area down the left side of the fairway. I almost pulled it off. My ball landed about where I had planned, but with a little too much hook spin. It took a hard kick to the left, coming to rest behind a pine tree in the rough.

"Well, if you had to hit one in the trees, this is probably a good time to do it," Herb opined as we walked off the tee. "You haven't hit this green in regulation all week. Hardest hole on the course for a short hitter. It's not like you just messed up a likely birdie opportunity."

"Not a bad way to look at it," I replied. "I recall Walter Hagen used to say he fully expected to hit about seven bad shots each round, so when he hit a bad one, he didn't get upset; he figured it was just one of the seven."

"There you go, Joe. You've come a long way. Staying philosophical about mistakes, not allowing them to derail your confidence or interfere with your focus—that goes a long way toward making you pressure-proof."

As we arrived at my ball, the good news was the lie. It was sitting cleanly up on the pine straw, and neither my backswing nor my follow-through would be impeded by nearby trees. The bad news was the large pine tree about ten feet in front of me, directly on my line to the green. We considered the options of pitching out directly sideways back into the fairway or shaping a low, hard running hook around the tree toward the green.

"Let's go with the hard hook," Herb recommended. "You have practiced shaping shots for months, and the Hook Hotch is perfectly suited for this shot. If we pitch back into the fairway, we are still left with around two hundred yards to a small, heavily bunkered green. If we can roll the ball up into one of the front bunkers, you should have a good lie in the sand, with a reasonable chance to get up and down for par. On the other hand, if we pitch out and go for the green from two hundred yards, there's a good chance you would fly it into one of the bunkers and be trying to get up and down for a five from a plugged lie."

I nodded in agreement and took the Hook Hotch from Herb. I closed the face a touch more than the built-in orientation, played the ball back in my stance, and hit a screaming hook that barely trickled into the front left bunker.

Herb applauded my effort. "Good damage control," he extolled. "Worst we can make now is a five."

"Yeah, but look what Wiley and Billy are up to!"

Wiley and Billy Dale were carefully surveying his second shot.

His gamble with the driver off the tee had paid off, leaving him with only 120 yards to the pin. He took his gap wedge from Wiley and hit a great shot. I watched in amazement as his ball almost hit the flag and stopped six feet below the hole.

Herb and I analyzed my bunker shot. The lie was no problem since my ball was sitting up cleanly on the sand. The pin, set in the front right of the green, was in a low spot, which would tend to gather the ball toward it. "This doesn't look all that difficult," Herb observed. "Just pop it up on the slope, and it should run down to the hole, like Tootie heading for her supper bowl. How's that for a visualization?"

For a brief instant, I had an image of Tootie scampering toward the hole, moving her short legs as fast as she could to propel her fat little body. I dug my feet in, opened the face of my sand wedge, and blasted the ball up on the green, spraying bright white sand up in a small cloud. The ball landed on the slope and took off toward the pin.

"Come on! Come on!" I whispered as I watched my ball. I almost shouted when I saw the ball go in—I had turned a likely bogey into an improbable birdie! Our gallery was as surprised as I was. Their reaction was more of a gasp than a roar. Most had been following our group to see Billy Dale Rankin claim his first major title, not witness the geezerfication of Augusta.

Billy Dale gave me a thumbs-up and turned his attention to his short birdie putt. He double-checked his read with Wylie and confidently stroked the ball into the cup.

The four of us were feeling pretty good about ourselves as we made our way from the seventh green to the eighth tee. I was certain that young Rankin was feeling especially confident because the eighth hole was a reachable par five for him. He had birdied the hole with easy two-putts in each of his first three rounds.

As we were waiting on the tee for the group ahead to clear the fairway, Herb reached into my bag and pulled out a small thermos. "It's approaching four, sir," he said with his best imitation of an English butler. "Would you care for a spot of tea, governor?"

I was tempted to tell him to drink all the tea himself and get me a cold beer in celebration of the lucky break at the last hole. Smiling at the thought of such a retort but opting to use better judgment, I answered with my own attempt to sound like an English lord. "Right oh, my good man. Jolly good show. I might fancy a crumpet or two as well."

"Your accent is even more pitiful than mine," Herb grimaced as he handed me the tea-filled lid of the thermos. "Let's make sure we don't get too carried away by our great fortune back there. It's just as important not to let good breaks interfere with your focus as it is not to allow bad shots to bother you. The only fairway bunker on this hole is out of our reach, so the tee shot is wide open for us. Nevertheless, don't get careless. Pick a precise target in the fairway and focus on it."

Rankin's birdie retained the honor for him. He was obviously feeling confident with his driver because he challenged the bunker on the right and hit a massive drive, which just cleared the far edge. His drive finished in position for him to easily reach the green on his second shot.

Taking Herb's advice, I focused my aim at a spot in the middle of the fairway and hit a respectable 245-yard drive into the uphill fairway.

"The field here gets stronger every year," Herb stated as he lugged my bag alongside me up the hill. "Not only do these younger players continue to get better and better; there is room in the field for more of them since not as many of the older champions take up spots anymore. One of the perks of winning the tournament is you get a lifetime invitation to come back and play every year. As time progressed, generating more and more champions, the spots being taken by the older past champions were increasingly limiting the number of spots available for younger, more competitive players. Some of the old guys were at the point where they couldn't break eighty anymore, but they still showed up every year to play. The tournament committee finally had to do something about the situation. They started sending a letter to the older past champions, strongly hinting they should consider giving up their spots. A number of the past champions voluntarily gave up their spots because they didn't want the embarrassment of getting 'the letter.' Several of them still show up for the par-three contest on Wednesday and hang around for the week, which is really fun for the fans. Nostalgia has always been a big part of the Masters. It is a win-win deal. The fans get to see the old guys, and the tournament is more competitive."

"I'm glad we didn't talk about that before we got here, Herb. It would have made me even more nervous," I replied as we arrived at my ball.

We looked over the second shot. No bunkers to worry about. Favoring the right side would give me a better angle to approach the pin. We decided on the Slice Hotch, choked halfway, hoping this would leave us a 110-yard pitch shot for our third. This was my most consistently accurate approach distance and usually resulted in a makeable birdie putt. I didn't adjust quite enough for the uphill stance, though, and came out of the shot slightly, resulting in a little more cut than we wanted. The ball landed a bit too far to the right and rolled just into the light rough.

"No major damage done," Herb whispered. "Rough over there isn't bad. With the pin in the back, we want the approach shot to run out a little anyway. This might work out better than trying to fly it all the way back there with spin from the fairway."

After watching Billy Dale hit a long iron to four feet short of the green, we marched up the hill to play my third shot.

"Just had an amusing thought," Herb chuckled as we strode toward my ball. "If you win this thing at your age, you might be the first winner who gets the trophy and 'the letter' simultaneously. Better check the inside pockets of the green jacket; it just might be in there. I can hear the club chairman's speech at the award ceremony: 'Mr. Goodman, we at Augusta National offer our sincere congratulations upon your victory. However, would you please consider not coming back to defend your title, as we need room in the field for younger, more competitive players?' That would be a great geriatric moment, don't you think?"

"You are a laugh riot, Herb," I answered with a fake growl. "Don't think I want to come back anyway. God didn't say anything about an encore."

My ball was lying nicely about a yard into the light rough, approximately 115 yards from the pin. The approach angle was just about perfect.

"All right," Herb said, surveying the shot. "We need to fly this shot 108 yards. It should release from there and run back near the hole. Let's go with your pitching wedge, square face, three-fourths choked, full swing."

I took a couple of practice swings, got a feel for the shot, and then made a smooth swing. I contacted the ball solidly, and the shot came off almost exactly as scripted. My ball landed short of the pin, released, and careened gently off the pin, settling about a foot away. I marked my ball for what would be an easy tap-in birdie.

With Wiley's encouragement, Billy Dale elected to putt from his position. They had read the speed and break almost perfectly. His ball finished on my ball marker. We both tapped in for our birdies, high-fived, and headed for the ninth tee.

The ninth hole was a long dogleg left par four. The tee shot was downhill, shortening the hole's effective length. The approach shot was played back uphill, to a green that sloped severely toward the front. Gauging distance on the approach shot was especially critical because balls landing short of the middle pin position often spun back off the green and continued running back down the fairway for twenty or thirty yards. Shots finishing above the pin were almost equally problematic, since the player was left with a treacherously fast putt.

Having matched me birdie for birdie on the previous two holes, Wiley's man still had the honor. He hit another superb tee shot, finishing at the bottom of the hill, leaving a flat lie for his approach shot.

"Try to hit this down the right side," Herb reminded me. "It takes the bunkers on the left side of the green more out of play."

I hit another good-for-an-old-guy drive, down the right side as instructed. However, with my lack of length, I didn't make it to the bottom of the hill. I was faced with the difficult task of a 180-yard approach from a downhill lie to an uphill target.

Herb gave me a pat on the back as I handed over my driver. "That's about as well as we could have expected," he said. "It's a good thing we spent all those hours working on hitting shots from downhill lies."

I knew that Herb was just trying to decompress me between shots. Another thought apparently came to him just then, which he shared, of course. "If you win and come back next year, they will expect you to plan the Champions Dinner," he speculated.

"Will you be quiet, Herb?"

Herb prattled on as if he hadn't heard me. "The defending champion always has the privilege of planning the menu for the past champions' dinner Tuesday evening at the club. What would be on your menu?"

"Probably something soft," I responded. "Most likely wash it down with prune juice, in keeping with my geezer motif. A lot of those past champions are a helluva lot older than me. They might appreciate those choices, especially the prune part."

"Maybe you could offer a blood transfusion as an appetizer and a laxative for dessert," Herb laughed. He seemed pleased with how readily he was able to keep me relaxed.

As we continued down the fairway, we heard an enthusiastic roar from the crowd around the eighth green, followed by a similar roar about a minute later. Apparently, both the leaders had birdied.

We decided not to get cute with the second shot—just hit it above the hole and try to two-putt. All the practice putting on the concrete floor in Herb's barn had given us a world of confidence in my speed control. I choked down on the Hook Hotch, aimed at the right edge of the green to take the bunkers out of play, and hit a high draw to about thirty feet above the hole.

Billy Dale and Wiley took a long time trying to figure out how to hit their shot the correct distance. They finally decided to hit a soft nine-iron. He could reach the pin with a full wedge, but the ball would probably have so much spin, it would back off the green. He made a decent pass at the ball, but as is common with shots players try to hit with less than full power, he didn't release the club head. The ball finished pin high, twenty feet right of the pin. They were left with an extremely difficult side-hill putt.

Herb and I looked over my putt. "Wow!" he commented. "Fastest putt I ever saw. After you marked your ball, I was half afraid your ball marker would start sliding down the slope. Wish we could put some chewing gum on your ball before you putt. Just trust yourself to get it right. Probably wouldn't hurt if you yelled 'Whoa' just as you hit it."

I hit maybe the best putt in my life. On three occasions, it appeared to have stopped cold, only to regain momentum, until it finally settled six inches past the hole. I hustled down the green and putted it in, before it could decide to take off again. The crowd applauded appreciatively. They were well aware of how difficult the putt was. Several players had putted their balls all the way off the green today from similar positions.

Billy Dale's putt was no bargain either. The twenty-footer had almost twenty feet of right-to-left break. His back to the hole, he hit a brave putt. It gained speed after it reached its apex and turned toward the hole. The putt was traveling much too fast. Miraculously, it hit the back of the cup, hopped out, and stopped just a foot away. He practically sprinted to the ball, tapped it in, and bowed to the crowd, setting off a good-natured round of applause. You couldn't have wiped the smile off Wiley's face with a Brillo pad. "Let's get out of here before they make us try those putts again," he gushed, jamming the flagstick back into the hole.

There was another delay at the tenth tee. Play was backing up a little as players negotiated the difficult back nine on the final round of the Masters. The swirling winds at Amen Corner required precise club selection. Unlike the par fives on the front side, the two par fives on the back presented classic risk-reward options, with water coming into play in front of both greens.

The back nine at Augusta on Sunday afternoon was not the time or the place to get into a hurry. Players with little or no chance to win the title were locked into the secondary battle to finish high enough to ensure an automatic invitation to next year's tournament. Every shot had to be well thought out. Patience was crucial.

I was munching on a banana when I heard polite applause coming from the ninth green. Both of the leaders had made relatively routine pars. Their well-placed approach shots had left them much less adventurous putts than Rankin and I had faced.

There were only four men in the field in red numbers. My thirty-four on the front put me at two under par for the tournament. With a bogey and a birdie apiece, the leaders stood where they had started the day, at four under par. Zane Campbell, in the group ahead, was having a fine round, shooting thirty-three on the front to get to one under par. Billy Dale had made up for most of his poor start and was at even par.

"Now the fun really begins," Herb advised as he washed down his own banana with a large swig of bottled water. "Embrace this moment. Keep playing the role of a confident, focused guy and let the other players deal with their self-generated pressure."

"I'm trying, Herb. Quit reminding me, okay? I get it!"

Herb shot me a worried look. "You're feeling the pressure."

I nodded. How could I not be feeling nervous? I was still in the running to win and didn't want to blow it. I knew there was no guarantee about anything, especially in golf, which made the uncertainty even more bothersome.

The tenth hole was traditionally the hardest hole on the course, and so it was no time for me to freeze up. From the tee, the 495-yard downhill par four resembled a ski run. The hole played much shorter if the drive found the steep bank on the left side of the fairway. Longer hitters frequently hit less than driver off the tee, shaping a draw to make sure they didn't overshoot the bank. Tee shots landing on the flatter right-hand side of the fairway didn't run nearly as far. Either way, the approach shot required hitting from a downslope to a demanding target. Adding to the difficulty were the subtle breaks of the green. Reading the green was especially tough since afternoon shadows from the pines on the right side made it hard to pick the correct line.

Billy Dale selected his three-wood to guard against hitting his ball through the dogleg and missing the left-side launching pad. He overcooked his draw slightly and was fortunate his ball stopped just short of the tree trouble along the left side. He had a clear line to the pin from a decent lie.

The drive did not present a clubbing option for me. I had to hit my driver as hard as I could to reach the slope—no danger of my going through the dogleg. I sauntered onto the tee, hitched up my pants in my best Arnold-Palmer-about-to-do-something-wonderful imitation, and hit a very serviceable shot. Not exactly the nice high draw I had envisioned, it was almost a snap hook. Fortunately, I had also managed to push it to the right, so the hook took it to a perfect landing place. It proceeded to bound down the fairway for my best result of the week off that tee.

"Got away with one there," Herb chuckled. "Let's confidently stride down the fairway acting as if that was just how you intended to play the shot. The announcers are probably saying something like 'Old Goodman may not be very long, but he really knows how to work his ball.' Keep smiling, and they'll never know the difference."

My second shot was still no bargain. I was left with 205 yards off a hanging lie, to a back right pin cut perilously close to the deep bunker on the right.

We didn't want any part of the bunker. No sense in taking a chance. Par was always a good score at the tenth. We selected the Slice Hotch, fully choked. I concentrated on keeping my balance and making solid contact from the difficult lie. I made a good pass at the ball, resulting in a medium-height fade. The ball started at the left center and cut its way to a spot thirty-five feet below the hole.

My long-hitting opponent had an eight-iron approach from a great angle. The lie would generate a draw. I couldn't hear what he and Wiley were saying, but I imagined Billy wanted to aim at the bunker and draw the ball toward the pin. Wiley probably talked him out of it. "There's an old adage in golf, kid," I imagined Wiley advising him. "Never aim at trouble because you might hit it straight." Whatever was said, Billy Dale played a slight cut to pin high, twenty feet left of the pin.

Putting through the moving shadows, neither of us managed to hole our putts. We had both overplayed the break, but our speed was good. We holed our simple par putts.

Herb patted me on the back as we made the trek through the tall pines over to the eleventh tee. "I'll take par there every time, especially on Sunday," he said. "Time to decompress. Let's talk about some sure signs an aging golfer isn't championship material anymore. For instance, you know you're not championship material anymore if you have to replace the grip on your ball retriever more than twice per season."

I snickered at the thought. "Or you know you're not championship material anymore if your preshot routine involves taking an aspirin?" I countered.

"How about, you know you're not championship material anymore if your caddy can hear your tee shots land?" Herb suggested.

"Okay," I continued. "You know you're not championship material anymore if you think your course needs more drivable par threes."

CHAPTER 10

||||||||||||||||||||||||||||||||||||||||||||||||||||||||||||||||||||||||||||||||||||||||||||||||||||||||||||||||||||||||||||||||||||||||||||

WE ARRIVED AT THE ELEVENTH TEE, STILL LAUGHING AND TRYING to come up with more silly signs indicating a golfer was no longer championship material. Herb was doing a great job of keeping me relaxed, despite my occasional bout with nerves. Staying relaxed was crucial as we faced the upcoming difficult three-hole stretch universally known as Amen Corner.

The tee on the eleventh had been moved farther back up the hill from its original location, lengthening the par four to over five hundred yards. Thank goodness it was downhill. In addition to its length, the hole presented one of the most difficult approach shots in championship golf. Shots landing even slightly left of optimum were gathered by the large pond to the left of the green. Ben Hogan, perhaps the best ball striker of all time, hadn't aimed at the eleventh green on his approach. He'd considered it too risky. Hogan had preferred to play his approach to the right of the green and try to get up and down for his par. He once remarked, "If you see my ball on the green in regulation on number 11, you'll know I pulled my second shot."

Long hitters aimed down the left side off the tee and hit a hard fade, allowing them more room for error. Billy Dale was certainly in the long-hitting category. He set up for a fade and hit a picture-perfect monster drive. The effort left him with only a short iron for his approach.

I didn't have the luxury of aiming left. The only way I could get to a reachable approach distance was to aim down the right rough line and hit a hard running draw. "Be sure to release the club head," Herb reminded me as he handed me the driver. I made a smooth swing, concentrating on keeping a light grip pressure, which promoted a full release. The resulting right-to-left ball flight turned out about as well as I could have expected. My ball tumbled down the fairway, finally stopping in the left edge, 220 yards from the green. "I'd have to say you are somewhat trainable," Herb told me as I handed over the driver. By Herb's standards, that was quite a compliment. I tipped my hat at him, doing my best impression of a touring pro nonchalantly responding to gallery applause.

The view as we descended from the tee was spectacular. White dogwoods camped under the towering pines along the fairway. Bright green fairways contrasted with dark areas under the trees. A kaleidoscope of colors from the gallery reflected off the water in front of the twelfth green at the bottom of the hill.

"As wonderful as this is, this isn't what golf is all about," reflected Herb, once again attempting to conserve my focus for shot making. "Too much emphasis is put on tournaments and the elite players. Real golf is about the inner essence of the game itself, especially all the lessons the game teaches us. It provides a microcosm of life, wherein we can get to know ourselves and our playing companions. Nowadays, most people ride carts, eliminating the interactions among players between shots. In my opinion, the best part of golf is the learning environment it can provide between parents and children. There's not enough of that happening nowadays. I almost never see a foursome made up of kids and their parents anymore. Most clubs could make better efforts at promoting junior golf. Maybe they have a once-a-year junior camp, or something like a father-son or mother-daughter tournament, but not like it ought to be."

"I couldn't agree more, Herb," I responded. "Some of my happiest childhood memories involve the times I spent playing golf with dad and my brothers. Dad taught us a whole lot more than just how to play the game. It was the perfect classroom for him to teach us life lessons about how to handle adversity as well as good fortune, how to deal with anger and frustration, how to interact with adults, and the importance of behaving honorably. I could go on for hours about this. I wish more parents and their kids were having the experience my dad had with his children. I'm proud our mission provided the opportunity to help Derek Finucane get back on track with his family situation."

"Probably could have mentioned this earlier," Herb admitted as we strode down the fairway, "but I received instructions about my next mission a couple of days ago. The boss wants me to head down to Texas next week. Oddly enough, the guy I'm supposed to work with is another banker named Joe. The guy has developed a new junior golf program designed around parents interacting with their kids. If we can get the program going, it should generate thousands of stories like yours and your dad's—maybe help a lot of families like Derek's as well."

I had known that Herb would not be a constant in my life and that he'd have to move on to help others. But hearing him say he would be leaving left me feeling a little deflated. His timing could have been better.

"You had to tell me this now?" I asked.

"God never gives you more than you can handle."

"So I've heard," I said.

We arrived at my ball and began plotting strategy for our approach shot. The menacing pond removed temptation to aim anywhere close to the flag.

"We've had good success getting up and down for par from the right-hand apron. No use changing our plan now," Herb advised. "Let's aim fifteen yards right of the green with the Hook Hotch. Concentrate on swinging out at the ball to avoid coming over the top. Increase the grip pressure in your left hand to keep the toe from turning over. That oughta produce a very slight draw working back toward the edge of the green."

"Sounds like a good plan to me," I agreed. "Who am I to argue with Ben Hogan?"

I took a couple of practice swings, acting as if I knew what I was doing. Completely immersed in playing the role of a great golfer, I made one of my best swings of the tournament. The shot took off on our target line and gently drew toward the right side of the green. I got a huge break. My ball landed on the side of an unseen undulation in the fairway. It kicked sharply to the left and ran across the green, stopping twelve feet below the hole. I did my best to look like a guy who had fully expected to hit a great shot as I handed the Hook Hotch back to Herb.

Herb was having none of it. "Much better to be lucky than to be good," he snorted. "You don't have to practice being lucky."

I had to agree with his observation.

Billy Dale Rankin was young, impulsive, and a trifle spoiled. He was, however, a good sport. He gave me one of those mock "I am not worthy" bows as Herb and I headed down the fairway to watch him play his approach. It was tempting to go at the pin from his position. He resisted and hit a very serviceable shot thirty feet right of the hole. The patrons applauded enthusiastically as we walked onto the green. We were the only twosome of the day who had both hit the green in regulation.

Heeding Wiley's advice to be cautious with the slick putt, Billy Dale hit a very commercial lag and tapped in for par.

Herb and I surveyed our birdie putt. There wasn't much break to it. We decided to play it just inside the right lip. Our read was perfect. I hit the putt a little softer than planned. It had just enough gas to get to the front of the hole and topple in, putting us at three under for the round and the tournament.

"Better leave before they arrest us for stealing that one!" Herb exclaimed as he replaced the pin and trotted off the green toward my bag.

Herb and I traversed the short distance to the twelfth tee. The huge gallery sitting on the hillside behind the tee was unusually quiet. They seemed stunned in the aftermath of what they had just observed, like witnesses to a horrific train wreck. One of the players in the group ahead of me, Zane Campbell, had been making the biggest charge of the day. After starting the round six strokes behind the leaders, he had just birdied the eleventh to go four under for the day. He had put himself in position to challenge for the title.

But the confidence generated by today's success had just overridden Zane's better judgment. He had taken dead aim at Sunday's sucker pin in the right corner of the green. The fickle Amen Corner breeze had come up on his backswing and knocked his ball down into Rae's Creek in front of the green. In a daze, he trudged down to the drop area and proceeded to hit two more balls in the creek; each time, the ball landed on the front of the green and spun back into the water. He finally got his third try on the green. We watched him two-putt for a sextuple-bogey nine, undoing all his previous good work. His chance for victory had drowned in the creek. The treacherous twelfth hole had struck again. Campbell would need to regroup and refocus on finishing high enough to earn an automatic invitation to next year's tournament.

We looked at the scoreboard behind the eleventh green just as the numbers were being updated. I got a little jolt as I saw Scott Thomas's score adjust from minus four to minus three. He had misread his long birdie putt through the shadows on ten, leaving him a six-foot comebacker. He had been unable to convert for par. I was now tied with him, and only one stroke behind Michael Cameron, who had managed to get up and down from the bunker for par at the tenth.

"Okay," Herb reassured me. "There's no pressure unless you manufacture it for yourself. We knew from day one the plan was for you to be in the hunt on the back nine Sunday afternoon, so there's no surprise here. Keep playing the role of a confident, relaxed golfer. Dial up the focus a little. Let's enjoy the ride."

Our birdie at eleven had given us the honor, which wasn't always a good thing at twelve. It was usually helpful to observe the wind's effect on your playing companion's shot to help you pick a club. However, we didn't need to discuss what shot we were going to play. Herb knew the swirling breeze at twelve could wreak havoc, even on a well-played shot, as evidenced by Zane Campbell's recent disaster. We had worked for long hours on Herb's range, perfecting a little cut-punch five-iron shot for this situation. The trajectory was low enough to minimize the effect of unexpected changes in the breeze. The cut spin mostly offset the run out from the line-drive flight pattern, preventing the ball from rolling through the green. Best of all, there was absolutely no indecision to disrupt my focus. We had decided how to play this shot long before arriving at Augusta.

I stepped into position and played the shot quickly. The announcers no doubt thought this was a sign of nervousness. They were accustomed to watching players and their caddies spend considerable time tossing pieces of grass in the air and debating how to play the shot. They didn't realize I knew only one way to play it. Sometimes it's good not to have options. My ball headed toward the green on its low trajectory, landing on the front edge thirty feet left of the hole. The cut spin applied the brakes and managed to stop the ball just short of the back edge. I patted my hand over my heart and did a fake stagger over to Herb, for the patrons' benefit. Most of them, as well as the announcers, thought I had skulled the shot and gotten away with it.

Wiley looked at me, nodding in appreciation. He knew I had pulled off a very crafty shot in a tough situation. The breeze was dying down slightly. Wiley handed Billy Dale his nine-iron, telling him to aim at the center of the green and hit quickly, before the wind came back up. Rushing the shot slightly, Billy Dale came over the top and pulled it to the left side of the green, leaving a long putt. "That's okay," Wiley encouraged. "We're dry. We can be heroes somewhere else."

"One helluva job you did with that tee shot," Herb whispered as we crossed the bridge over Rae's Creek. "It was exactly what we had on the drawing board."

"Most of the credit is yours," I replied, "not only for the hours you spent teaching me the cut punch, but also for the way you taught me to incorporate visualizing it in my morning meditations. When I stood over the ball, it felt as if I had already done this hundreds of times. It's

126

amazing how all you've taught me ties in together, especially changing my schedule. Changing my concept of a day, putting those hours I've gained in the morning to good use, has been a life-changer for me."

"How do you plan to use your morning hours once this is done?"

"I've given it a little thought. Maybe I'll use the time to write a book about this experience. Maybe I'll tinker with some inventions I've had in the back of my mind for years. Now that I am more aware of how God communicates with us, I am sure I'll receive some guidance pointing me in the right direction."

We were silent for a few moments. Then I said, "I'm going to miss you, you know."

"For a guy with a banker's brain, you are making remarkable progress," Herb laughed, ignoring what I'd just said. "Makes me wonder how much a guy with a full-size brain could accomplish. Okay, back to business: let's figure out how we can two-putt this nasty downhill bugger."

Wiley tended the pin as Billy Dale stroked his incredibly difficult putt. Demonstrating an amazing sense of touch for a big guy, he coaxed his ball across the green to within a foot of the hole. He sighed in relief, tapped in, and waved to the large crowd behind the tee. Wiley patted him on the back in congratulations. "We dodged a bullet there, Hoss," he sighed.

The concrete barn floor practice and body-putting technique combined to allow me to two-putt my difficult downhiller. Herb and I were very pleased to par the tricky hole.

As we left the green, we heard a groan from behind us. Cameron had missed his par putt on eleven.

I was tied for the lead. I tried not to think about that as Herb and I climbed up the thirteenth tee located in the woods above the twelfth green. It was the only tee box on the course that was inaccessible to the gallery. The four of us enjoyed the relative privacy for a few minutes.

The hole was a dogleg par five, reachable in two shots by most of the field. There was usually a delay on the tee while the players in the fairway waited for the green to clear. Herb didn't want me to start overthinking our situation during this delay in the action. "We've been on quite a ride this past year, haven't we?" he asked as he handed me an apple to munch on. "Lots of wonderful things have happened, not all of them related to golf."

"Lots of amazing stuff," I agreed. "I get a buzz every time I think about Mary Garcia and Farrah. What a wonderful miracle!"

The fairway cleared. I reluctantly returned to the present. Once again my lack of length was sort of an advantage. Most of the players felt compelled to reach the green in two. This entailed having to shape their tee shot right to left, to avoid hitting through the fairway into a grove of pine trees. This was somewhat risky because shots hit too far to the left splashed into a small tributary of Rae's Creek; the small stream meandered down the left side of the hole before crossing the fairway just in front of the green. No problem for me. I couldn't reach the trees unless my ball landed on a rock, and there weren't any rocks in the fairways at Augusta National. I took a few extra practice swings to overcome the small amount of stiffness resulting from sitting on my bag for several minutes. My swing still reflected a little latent stiffness. I caught the ball slightly thin, but it didn't matter much. It stopped in the fairway about twenty yards short of what would have been my best effort. No problem. My plan was to lay well back with my second shot.

Billy Dale and Wiley concurred on a slightly risky tee shot. He could easily reach the green in two after a well-placed drive. The required right-to-left shot fit his natural shot pattern. He hit a powerful draw, starting over the right side of the fairway. The ball landed in the middle and scampered along, finally coming to rest a few feet inside the left fairway line about 190 yards from the green.

We strode from the tee. Thomas and Cameron were exiting the twelfth green. As might be expected from two veteran pros, they had played the hole sensibly and walked away with easy pars.

I played the rest of the thirteenth almost exactly as planned. Herb and I carefully calculated the distance for my lay-up second shot, leaving my favorite 110-yard distance for the approach. From there,

I hit a nice little pitching-wedge shot to six feet and made the putt for my birdie.

Billy Dale played the hole almost perfectly. His second shot was a high cut into the middle of the green. Wiley gave him a great read on the putt. Billy Dale stroked it squarely into the back of the cup. He was one happy man as he exited the green, acknowledging the patrons' deafening cheers for his eagle.

We walked over to the fourteenth tee, the cheers for Rankin's eagle still ringing in our ears. Herb was doing everything in his power not to mention I had the lead. But as much as people prefer to ignore the elephant in the room, usually it's impossible. "Think it'll rain?" he said, grinning foolishly and pointing at the cloudless sky.

"Nice try," I replied. "But now that we're in the lead, you'll have to come up with something better than that. This is starting to get pretty intense."

One of the most difficult challenges of competitive golf is how to deal with the numerous breaks in the action. Only a small portion of the time spent in a round entails actual shot-making. The long stretches of time between shots afford ample opportunity for the wrong stuff to creep into a player's mind. I could feel my heart pounding, could almost hear it thrumming in my inner ear. I knew I was in a position to win the Masters, and I knew God wanted me to, but it was up to me to get the job done. God wasn't going to hit the shots for me or nudge my ball into the hole. I reminded myself that all I could do was keep playing my best and maintain faith that I could win. That's what life is all about: try your best and see what happens. Mostly, precisely what you think will happen never does, but things work out.

Billy Dale's previous eagle gave him the honors on the fourteenth hole. Obviously pumped up, he had teed his ball and was now pacing around the tee box. Our two one-putts on the previous green had not taken much time. The group ahead of us was still marching toward their drives. Wiley tried to get his man to sit down and relax, but he continued to pace around the tee, anxious to get moving. He had crept to within two shots of the lead and didn't want to lose his momentum.

Wiley sided up to us. "Don't know how I'm going to get my guy to settle back down," he whispered. "The poor start may have been a blessing. It got him out of thinking about winning. Now that he's back in the hunt, he's beginning to feel the pressure again. Can't say I blame him. The golf writers have been picking him to win all week. One of them came up to him on the practice range this morning and asked if the tournament committee knew his correct jacket size, so they would have a perfect fit ready for him this afternoon. He should have just ignored the guy. He told the reporter to tell them he was a size 46 long. After the first two holes, he told me he wished he hadn't answered the guy. He could imagine the headline, describing him as an overconfident choker."

"I've had my own green jacket fantasy since I was a kid," I whispered back. "Like most young golfers, I used to imagine winning the Masters. When the previous year's winner put the green jacket on me, I'd button it up, tell him it was a nice fit, and—being the little wise guy I was—ask if he had the same thing in navy blue."

In trying to stifle a laugh, Wiley went into a snorting fit. I thought he was going to hurt himself. Herb loaned him a handkerchief to clean up his beard. Billy Dale turned around, obviously irritated at having his concentration broken by our antics. Wiley waved him off and pointed down the fairway, where the group ahead was just moving out of range.

There was a fair amount of applause coming from the thirteenth green. Both Cameron and Thomas had successfully hit the green with their second shots. The patrons were applauding their efforts as they strode onto the putting surface.

The fourteenth hole appeared somewhat benign from the tee because it was the only hole on the course that didn't have bunkers. It didn't need any. The green was extremely difficult, providing more than enough challenge itself. A slightly misplayed approach shot would leave the golfer with a chip or putt that was almost impossible to get down in two.

Frowning with concentration, Billy Dale addressed his teed ball.

He hit a hard smash down the right side. The ball failed to execute its customary draw back to the middle. His mental state had led Billy Dale to grip a fraction too tightly, preventing his normal release. The ball hung out on its line down the right and settled into the rough, behind a group of trees.

The navy-blue story had done its job. Still smiling, I took a couple of relaxed practice swings and hit a smooth drive to the left center of the fairway.

We trekked down the fairway toward our drives, trying carefully to pace ourselves. Many times in previous situations, Herb had cautioned me to walk slowly. "If you walk fast, it creeps into the rest of your game," he warned.

I heard enthusiastic cheers and then groans and polite applause from the thirteenth green, followed shortly by a similar sequence of sounds. Cameron and Thomas had narrowly missed their eagle putts and easily tapped in for birdies. The three of us were now tied for the lead at four under par.

"Okay, let's see if I can come up with something better than the weather to talk about," Herb mused. "Here's a good one. When it is all said and done, what do you want the person doing the eulogy to say at your funeral?"

"How about 'Look! He just moved! He's not really dead!'"

"Very funny," Herb deadpanned. "Maybe I don't have to worry so much about keeping you loose. You're doing a pretty darn good job on your own."

"Yeah, and maybe I'm just whistling as I walk by the graveyard. I'm just doing the best I can to act like someone who is relaxed and confident."

"Then you oughta get an Oscar for this performance. If I didn't know any better, I'd think you actually were relaxed and confident. Speaking of whistling, let's borrow a page from Farrah's playbook."

Without attracting attention, we softly whistled the rousing Beethoven tune all the way to my ball and began planning the approach shot. The pin was cut in the back middle. I was facing almost exactly two hundred yards. After the group ahead cleared, Herb handed me the Slice Hotch, suggesting I choke down to the first mark on the grip. I caught the ball solidly and hit a little fade starting left of the pin and cutting to a spot twenty feet directly below the cup. Very serviceable.

Billy Dale had only 140 yards to the green but was blocked by pine trees. After discussing his options with Wiley, he took out a five-iron and hit a very classy low punch shot that finished only a foot off the left side of the green.

Unfortunately, his third shot was almost impossible. He elected to putt from the fringe. His attempt looked promising at first, as it glided up the hump in the green, but ran out of steam about ten feet short of the hole and trickled back down the slope, finally stopping five feet below my ball marker. He gathered himself and managed to hit a very good second putt, which rimmed out and left him on the lip for a bogey. Considering the mistake with his drive and the weak first putt, it wasn't a bad bogey.

My playing companion's misfortune was my good fortune. His second putt gave me the exact read for my birdie putt. Perhaps a little overconfident with the read, I hit my putt too firmly. Luckily, it hit the back of the hole, jumped six inches in the air, and fell in.

"Somebody should give the hole a Gold Glove Award for that catch," Herb muttered as we quickly beat a path toward the fifteenth tee.

CHAPTER 11

||||||||||||||||||||||||||||||||||||||||||||||||||||||||||||||||||||||||||||||||||||||||||||||||||||||||||||||||||||||||||||||||||||||||||||||||||||||||||||||||||

AS HAD BEEN THE CASE AT THE PREVIOUS PAR FIVE. THERE WAS another considerable delay at the fifteenth tee. The players in the group ahead of us were leaving the tee as we arrived. Upon reaching their drives, both elected to go for the green with their second shots and stood waiting in the fairway for the green to clear.

"Might as well get comfortable," Herb advised as he set my bag down. "These reachable par fives are dramatic, but they almost always cause bottlenecks."

Billy Dale's bogey at fourteen had thrown cold water on the euphoria created by his eagle at thirteen. Wiley managed to get him to sit down for a little chat. Four strokes down with four holes to go, he would likely need another eagle, plus a couple of birdies, to have a chance. Wiley did not want him to press too hard on this tee shot. He could easily reach the green from the distance his normal drive would leave him. Billy Dale had a tendency to turn his natural draw into a hook when he tried for extra distance. A hooked drive would likely finish behind the grove of trees to the left, blocking his second shot.

Herb was giving me a shoulder rub as we stood on the opposite side of the tee from our playing companions. My back muscles had tightened a bit while we waited on the thirteenth tee. This delay would likely last at least ten minutes, which was ample time for an old geezer like me to stiffen up. The physical and mental demands of four consecutive days of intense competition were beginning to wear on me. I hoped I had enough gas in the tank to get to the finish line.

"The conversation with God on Saturday afternoon before we left really helped," I reflected. "I was worried about being able to handle all the questions people might have of me if I won. Now I know I'll have all the help I need. God gave me a great answer about evolution. Kind of wish I had asked Him a few more questions, though."

"Like what?"

"I am still struggling with why bad things happen to seemingly good people. Like Mary Garcia's family, for instance. I got quite a bit of comfort last fall from your Persian rug analogy, but it still bugs me. Atheists use this as a prime justification for not believing. I've never heard a priest, or anybody, give an explanation that refutes the atheists' position. Have you got anything else to offer me here?"

"Like I said last fall, I'm not sure there's an explanation that can be understood at the human level," Herb replied. "You need to have faith in eventually ascending to a higher level of understanding. Sounds like you've given the question some more thought, though. What have you come up with?"

"I know how ridiculous it is to plug a banker-size brain into this question, but could it be because we were not created as robots? We were given the power of choice, and sometimes our choices are wrong, leading to dire consequences? Could it be that in the context of eternity, our little life spans aren't even a drop in the ocean, so in the grand scheme of things, what happens during our short lifetimes is rather inconsequential? Could it be reincarnation exists, allowing us to go through many lifetimes in our development, and part of the development process is for us to experience and learn from lifetimes that are tragic? Could it be God created the physical world, set it in motion, and chooses not to interfere with any of the ongoing physical realities, such as gravity, earthquakes, tornadoes, slippery roads, engine failures, et cetera? Maybe he restricts His involvement to things that are spiritual in nature. Could it be He does not prevent tragedies but rather provides the spiritual strength to deal with them? Could it be the purpose of tragedies is to test our faith? To make us stronger?"

"Uh-oh. Could it be that we are going to get a two-stroke penalty for slow play if we don't snap out of this and hit our tee shot?" Herb asked, spotting a rules official walking toward us, anxiously tapping on his watch.

"Guess that guy just doesn't understand how close a couple of geniuses like us were to solving one of the great mysteries of the universe," I said with a grin as Herb handed me my driver. Rushing a little to humor the official, I hurried my routine and hit a bit more of a hook than planned. My ball rolled into the light rough just left of the fairway. No real problem. I had no intention of going for the green on my second shot. The lie in the left rough was an easy spot to play my planned lay-up second.

Wiley had successfully managed to bring his man into the proper frame of mind. Resisting the urge to murder the ball, Billy Dale put a smooth swing on it and hit another of his patented high draws down the right side of the fairway. It finished in the middle, not more than midiron distance from the green.

As we prepared to chase after our tee shots, Cameron and Thomas sauntered onto the tee. Both had made rather uneventful routine pars on fourteen. They sat on their bags, resigned to the interruption in play. Cameron's caddy, Tracy "Big Dog" Hooker, was an old friend of Wiley's. I overheard him as he squinted down the fairway and asked Wiley, "Did Herb's man finally miss a fairway?"

"Yes, he did," replied Wiley, winking at me. "Wasn't easy. It takes a lot of talent to be both short and crooked." We all got a good laugh out of that as we headed down the fairway.

"Ever think God may have created us just for his own amusement?" I postulated as we trudged along.

"Well, you gotta admit we have been pretty darn entertaining," Herb replied. "What with going over Niagara Falls in barrels, bungee jumping, the Hula-Hoop, and countless other examples of nonsense, we have been rather fun to watch. If I had to take a serious stab at explaining why He made us, I'd guess it would be so that we could glorify Him, as well as to experience life through us, in order to broaden His own perspective."

I chewed on that as we continued down the fairway. It made about as much sense as any other explanation I had heard about the meaning of life.

Arriving at my ball, Herb and I did some quick math. We wanted to leave a third shot at my favorite distance of 110 yards. We calculated our distance to the pin at 282 yards. Considering the downslope in front of the green and the possibility of catching a flier from our lie, we elected to go with a seven-iron for my lay-up. "Remember to focus on an exact target, Joe," Herb cautioned. "It's easy to lose focus when all you are trying to do is lay up. This shot has to finish just left of the middle to give you a good angle for our third. Aim about five yards left of those trees on the right side and hit a little draw."

"Darn. Where's that fat guy with the red shirt when I need him?" I asked. "Probably too much to expect him to wander down here and stand in the fairway for me. I guess those trees will have to do for a target."

I carefully lined up to our target, went through my routine, and hit a stock seven-iron, drawing the ball to almost exactly the spot we'd planned.

Billy Dale waited by his ball for the green to clear. He was debating with Wiley over club selection. They finally decided on a five-iron, aimed at the middle of the green, hoping to cut it slightly toward the pin. He made several rehearsal swings and, once the green cleared, hit a great shot, leaving him about twelve feet for his eagle attempt.

We admired Billy Dale's shot as we ambled along toward my modest lay-up. Reversing roles, I initiated our decompression with a question. "Think you'll get into Heaven, Herb? Considering all the missions you've been on, God would likely give you a pretty high grade."

"Not sure He grades us. If He does, it is probably on some sort of curve."

"Curve? That sounds sort of scary to me. Be just my luck to be in line outside the Pearly Gates and find out I'm right behind a couple of folks like Mother Teresa or Billy Graham. I wouldn't look too good when it came my turn. I should probably wait around for a politician or a lawyer to show up and sneak into line right behind one of them."

"That'd probably increase your chances," Herb said with a grin as he set my bag down by our ball.

My third shot was from a good angle but was by no means easy. A major downside to playing it safe with a lay-up second was that the third shot must be played from a severe downslope. Perceived pressure and a downslope combined to create a perfect recipe for a mishit wedge shot. There have been many sad stories of players ruining their chance for victory by dumping their third shot on the fifteenth hole into the pond fronting the green. Herb and I had known in advance that we would be facing this challenge four times during the tournament since we had no choice but to lay up. In preparation, Herb had mowed a special portion of his practice range very tightly and carved it to a slope even steeper than the lay-up area on fifteen. We had practiced for hours, until I could consistently make good contact from the difficult lie.

"Okay, Joe," Herb said reassuringly as he pulled the pitching wedge out of my bag, "just like we've practiced. Play it back in your stance. Focus on just the front portion of the ball. Act as if you have done this a million times."

"As hard as we worked on this on your range, I feel like I've done it at least a million times," I replied. I gripped down to the three-quarters position and put a full, firm swing on the ball. Contact was solid. The ball took off on a relatively low trajectory with lots of spin. It landed two feet above the hole and spun back to four feet below. I got a great patron response. Many of them at fifteen were veteran spectators. They knew how difficult that wedge shot was.

Wiley could barely keep up as Billy Dale, clearly pumped up again, almost trotted up to the green. He caught up with the contender at the back of the green. I saw him waving his index finger at Billy, and I imagined what he was saying as Herb and I closed the distance between us: "I'm not going to hand you this putter until you take five deep breaths and get yourself calmed down a little."

We were almost at the green when I saw Billy Dale nod at his caddy. After a breathing exercise, they walked onto the green, marked his ball, and began reading the putt. Purposefully taking their time, they got everything right. The patrons went bonkers as his ball rolled into the cup for his second eagle on the back nine.

My four-footer normally would have been simple, and thanks to Herb, it was. He made sure I kept it simple. Herb reminded me to just focus on my routine and act like a guy who made four-footers on the last round of the Masters every day. I body-putted the ball firmly into the back of the cup. "This can't be as easy as we made it look," I whispered to Herb as he replaced the pin.

"Yeah," he replied. "They should flash a sign across the TV screen to warn viewers not to try this at home. These tricks are being performed by highly trained, paid professionals."

An enormous roar erupted from the sixteenth hole. The patrons perched on the hillside along the left side of the famous par three were going crazy. Zane Campbell had just made a hole in one! His ball had landed slightly above the hole to the right and motored down the slope into the cup.

"He might be the most improved par-three player in the world," Herb suggested. "A nine on twelve and then a one on sixteen. Average still isn't that hot, though—works out to be double-bogey, if you do the math."

I was happy for Zane. Following his disaster at twelve, he had rallied to birdie thirteen and fifteen. With the hole in one at sixteen, he was now even par for the tournament. Barring another disaster, he should finish high enough to earn an automatic invitation to next year's tournament.

We were a happy little group as we made our way to the sixteenth tee. Billy Dale and I had played fifteen exactly as planned.

Zane's good fortune had given everyone a positive buzz. For once, we didn't have a long wait at the tee. The group ahead of us may have set the all-time record for playing the sixteenth hole quickly. Following Zane's ace, his playing partner had almost followed suit, hitting a great shot to within a foot of the cup. He quickly strode across the green, tapped in, and headed for the seventeenth tee.

Behind us we heard a cheer for Michael Cameron's second shot into fifteen. It landed in the middle of the green and bit nicely, leaving him a reasonable chance for an eagle. Seconds later, the patrons groaned as Scott Thomas's attempt failed to clear the pond.

At our own tee, Herb and I could both see that Wiley was pretending to have trouble calculating the distance. He was trying to buy some time to calm down young Mr. Rankin. The eagle on the fifteenth hole, along with the electric atmosphere surrounding the sixteenth, had Billy Dale a little too pumped up.

Herb put his arm around my shoulders. "Joe, before it gets too crazy, I just want to tell you how proud I am of you. The wedge shot you just hit into fifteen was a true culmination of everything we've worked toward. Nobody could have pulled that shot off any better than you did. The hours and hours of practice have been extremely demanding, the morning mental sessions even more so. But you have hung in there."

"You deserve most of the credit," I replied. "Without you I would not have had a clue about where to start. The Big Guy knew what He was doing when He selected you to be my guru."

"I guess I can claim part of the credit, but you're the one hitting the shots. As they say, when the student is ready, the teacher will appear. You are an exception to most folks. The old adage 'give a man a fish, and you've fed him for a day; teach a man to fish, and you've fed him for life' isn't as true now. Nowadays, it's more like 'teach a man to fish, and then you have to give him worms.' Not many people with gumption anymore."

"Let's see if I can summon up enough gumption to hit this green. Not much of an advantage for us to watch the kid hit his shot. Hard for me to club off a guy who can spit farther than I can hit a nine-iron."

Herb feigned indignation. "I can't believe you just said that. A little crude for a guy on a mission from God, don't you think?"

"Just trying to keep it loose and relaxed, boss. Besides, nobody heard it but you, and you're awfully hard to offend."

I nudged Herb and nodded toward Wiley. The wise caddy dutifully guided Billy Dale through another breathing exercise and then handed him his seven-iron once he appeared sufficiently relaxed. The seven-iron was an excellent choice. Billy Dale's ball landed almost exactly where Zane's had a few minutes earlier, trickled down the slope, kissed off the side of the pin, and stopped four feet below the cup.

The patrons were understandably excited about seeing a hole in one and two near misses over the past few minutes. I could hear shouts of "Hole it!" as Herb and I sized up our shot.

"Let's swallow our pride and hit a very conservative shot here," Herb cautioned.

"No problem," I replied. "I have always taken great pride in my lack of pride."

Herb snickered and handed me my five-iron. We knew we couldn't get as high as the pin with the five, but using the five-iron eliminated the chance of going above the hole, leaving a very nasty downhill putt. We would rather be forty feet short than half that distance above the hole. I caught the ball solidly and did a little better than expected, leaving me twenty-five feet below the cup. Although Herb and I were very pleased with the shot, it generated little patron reaction. After the last three shots they had witnessed, mine was remarkably unspectacular. For the gallery's sake, I tried to look disappointed in my effort as Herb and I approached the green.

We heard polite applause, followed by a gasp from the crowd around the fifteenth green. Cameron had hit a very commercial lag for his eagle attempt. It never scared the hole but left a simple tap-in for his birdie. He was only a stroke behind me. Thomas's troubles continued. After taking a drop, he hit a respectable pitch to about five feet, giving him a chance to escape with par. Uncharacteristically, he misread the short putt. It spun out of the hole, leaving him with a bogey on a hole he had banked on birdieing.

My uphill putt was an easy read. Speed was the issue. We did not want to run by the hole and leave a tricky downhill comebacker. Herb advised me to picture the hole as being about two feet short of its actual location. Slightly anxious, I came up a little and didn't catch the ball solidly. It hopped a couple of times in the first few feet, stopping just outside my playing companion's ball marker—the dreaded "you didn't lose your turn" scenario.

"Don't mark your ball," Herb advised. "Just walk up there cool as a cucumber and body-putt it in before you have a chance to think about it." Once again, Herb's advice was spot-on. I holed the putt, looking to the world like I was as unconcerned as a guy playing his pal for a beer at his local course.

My putt gave Billy Dale the exact line for his birdie effort. Confident with the line, he stroked his ball smoothly into the cup.

"Thanks for the assist," Wiley said, grinning, as we exited the green.

"Yeah, I'd like to tell you that I'm such a fine sportsman, I topped my first putt on purpose," I replied, smiling and shaking my head. "My nose might grow about a foot if I did."

CHAPTER 12

||||||||||||||||||||||||||||||||||||||||||||||||||||||||||||||||||||||||||||||||||||||||||||||||||||||||||||||||||||||

T HE GROUP AHEAD OF US WAS PREPARING TO HIT THEIR APPROACH shots as we walked onto the seventeenth tee. Their quick completion of the sixteenth had created a little separation.

Although the seventeenth was a relatively straight hole, the tee shot played like a slight dogleg left because of the large pine tree in the left side of the fairway. Even casual fans knew the history of the tree. When the late President Eisenhower was a member at Augusta National, he always had difficulty playing the seventeenth. The General generally sliced his drives. The tree would not allow him to aim down the left to accommodate his ball flight. He reportedly lobbied to have the tree removed, but to no avail. President Eisenhower was long gone now, but the tree was still flourishing.

In spite of Wiley's efforts to slow him down coming off the sixteenth green, Billy Dale grabbed his driver and practically sprinted to the tee. After convincing him to go through the breathing routine again, Wiley walked to the rear of the tee to converse with Herb.

"Don't know why my man is so jumpy about winning this thing. Billy Dale was born on third base. He doesn't have to hit a triple. He is from a wealthy oil family in Texas. His wife is the former Jane Graciella, Miss Texas in the Miss USA Pageant a few years ago. His endorsement deals with major golf companies generate over four million a year. I reminded him to relax. His life is pretty darn good even if he doesn't win the tournament."

"Hard not to envy a guy like that," Herb acknowledged. "But at the same time you gotta admire someone who has all that going for him and still wants to test himself. Playing the tour can be a grind. It would be tempting to stay home with your beautiful wife and just count your money."

When the fairway cleared, Billy Dale teed his ball, waggled a couple of times, and hit a big cut over the Eisenhower Pine. It landed in the middle of the fairway over three hundred yards from the tee.

I didn't have the option of hitting a towering shot over the pine tree. My only route was to tee my ball on the left side of the box, aim well to the right of the tree, and hit a draw. I managed to pull the shot off as planned, leaving me on the left side of the fairway, 205 yards from the green.

Walking up the fairway, Herb looked around, trying to take it all in. "Kinda wish Sheila and Tootie were here to see all this," he said, once again attempting to disengage me from my shot focus.

"As much as I would like to have Sheila here, she's involved with something much more important this afternoon," I countered. "She invited our kids to come over to watch the broadcast. Our plan was for her to tell them the whole story about the mission while they watched their old man try to win the Masters. One of the biggest regrets of our lives has been our inability to pass our faith on to our kids. If we ever have grandkids, I just hate the thought of their not being raised in a strong faith environment. I thought we were doing reasonably well with our kids' spiritual lives until they went to college. They really drifted away from church while they were gone. They rarely attend at all anymore."

"Unfortunately, your scenario isn't all that uncommon," Herb replied, shaking his head. "Young people have a propensity to be a little rebellious at that stage of their lives. Then there is the natural tendency for college students to be somewhat in awe of their professors, who may have the idea that they are too smart to believe in anything that can't be empirically proven. Many believe their six or seven years of postgraduate education trumps the wisdom of the ages.

"Students can be inclined to believe their professors' opinions about issues such as religion and politics. Many professors don't have much real-world experience. They have spent their entire lives in the academic womb, merely making a one-time transition from the back of the classroom as students to the front of the classroom as teachers. They can be woefully inadequate outside the academic arena. Without you there, your kids don't get reinforcement of traditional values. A lot of your good work can be undone in a short while."

"I've thought all along, one of the best things about this mission is the possibility of reconnecting my kids with the church."

"Let's take another step in that direction with a good approach shot here," Herb responded as he set my bag down to the right of my ball. Then he said just loud enough for me alone to hear, "Oh, yeah. I'll miss you too."

I smiled broadly and looked out at the gallery. Patrons were vacating their spots along the holes behind us as the last group finished each hole. Looking back down the fairway, I saw Cameron and Thomas walk onto the tee. Thomas had birdied the sixteenth, bringing him to four under. Cameron had two-putted for par, leaving him at five under.

We decided to go with the Slice Hotch, hoping to hit a high fade to the middle of the green. The pin was cut dangerously close to the gaping bunker in front. We decided it would be better to face a lengthy putt than risk a plugged lie in the bunker. I took the club from Herb and settled into the shot. My focus slipped ever so slightly, and I caught the ball thin, sending it off on a much lower trajectory than we had envisioned. Human beings aren't perfect, but occasionally we get lucky. Almost as if it had a mind of its own, the ball landed on an upslope just left of the bunker and popped up on the green about thirty feet left of the flag. As we stared in disbelief, Wiley looked over at Herb, pinching his nose as if suddenly confronted with a foul odor.

"Just like over at eleven. We'd rather be lucky than good," Herb said, smiling at Wiley. "Lots less work. You don't have to practice being lucky!"

The exchange between our caddies appeared to relax Billy Dale.

He took dead aim and almost holed his soft nine-iron shot. The ball landed a foot from the hole and stopped stone-dead.

"Got to credit your superior experience on that one, Mr. Weaver," Herb joked as the four of us trudged onto the green. "Joe and I never would have thought about simply hitting a high shot right at the pin. We put our heads together and decided the best plan was just to skull a low one in the general direction of the green and see what happened."

Wiley snorted in reply and removed the flag, allowing Billy Dale to tap his ball in for the easy birdie.

My putt was fast, but not as fast as it would have been had I hit the shot to the middle of the green as planned. Herb and I agreed on the line. He wanted me to focus on a light grip pressure to maintain my sense of touch. He didn't want a repeat of the tension I had let creep in on the approach shot. "Light grip and complete confidence," Herb whispered as I took a couple of practice strokes. I hit the putt on the line we had picked. It was scary for a moment when it looked as if I had not hit the ball nearly hard enough. I walked along, mentally urging the ball from behind as it continued to trickle and trickle. It finally stopped just short of the lip on the low side. I was glad not to have to battle with a tricky par putt at this stage in the round. Heaving a sigh of relief, I tapped it in. Attempting to look casual, I nonchalantly flipped my putter to Herb.

The four of us stood on the eighteenth tee, gasping for breath. I knew it was my imagination, but it seemed as if the gallery had inhaled all the available oxygen. Now that the action was reduced to the two remaining holes, hundreds of patrons were crammed into a relatively small area.

As we waited for the fairway to clear, Cameron and Thomas both hit decent approach shots onto the seventeenth green, leaving them reasonable chances for birdies.

"Let's make this interesting," suggested Wiley, no doubt attempting to relax his man. "Wanna play this hole for a beer?"

"Only if you give us a stroke," Herb countered. "The way Billy Dale has played the last five holes, it seems only fair."

This produced fake smiles all around. We recognized it was going to take a lot more than a feeble attempt at humor to equip us to handle the task at hand.

Billy Dale's birdie at the previous hole put him at five under for the tournament, only a shot back of my six-under lead. He teed his ball and walked over to shake my hand. "Whatever happens here, Joe, I want you to know that playing this round with you and Herb has been an incredible experience. I don't think I could have recovered from my horrendous start if I had been paired with anyone else. You've both taught me a lot today."

He stepped up to his ball and pounded a high fade that started at the fairway bunkers on the left side and curved beautifully to the middle of the fairway. He had taken a chance by hitting a driver because it put the bunkers in play. Many of the longer hitters hit three-wood at the eighteenth hole, to play short of the bunkers. With a stroke to make up, Billy Dale and Wiley thought it worth the risk. Their gamble had paid off. The monster drive left them only 155 yards for their approach on the 465-yard uphill hole.

Hitting a driver was not a gamble for me since I couldn't reach the fairway bunkers. I planned to aim at them. A little cut wouldn't hurt because it would ensure staying out of the rough down the left side.

"There's no pressure here unless you think there is," Herb advised. "Just need to pretend this is no sweat for you. Focus on keeping your grip light with your left hand slightly tighter than your right, so the ball won't go left. Try not to break wind at impact."

"Perfect," I replied. "Very appropriate. A wind-related tip from an old windbag."

Smiling at my twenty-watt-bulb attempt at repartee, I relaxed as much as possible and hit maybe the best drive of my life. It was a hard line drive to the left side of the fairway, about five yards short of the bunkers.

Herb was about to tell me something when a deafening roar erupted from the seventeenth green. One of our pursuers had made his birdie putt. Which one? If it was Cameron, he had just tied me for the lead. A birdie by Thomas would put him at five under, tied with Billy Dale and Cameron. Several reporters joined our group as we walked up the steep fairway. Most of them wore headsets in order to exchange information with their colleagues around the course. One of them got our attention and signaled "five-five" with his outstretched palms to indicate Thomas had birdied, and both he and Cameron were at five under par.

Herb and I sighed in relief. At least we were still in the lead. If we could avoid a bogey at eighteen, the other three players would have to birdie to catch us.

"One last focus decompression," Herb wheezed. "Tell me who is better off, the man who has the most or the man who needs the least?"

"Let's see," I muttered, pondering the question. "Okay, my guess is it would be the man who needs the least because he doesn't have to worry as much as the guy who has to take care of all his stuff."

"Correct, banker man!" Herb replied. "Simple is always better. When you leave this world, you're not taking any material goods with you. Might as well learn not to need them. You have come a long way. You could be the world's smartest banker!"

"Isn't that like being the world's tallest pygmy? Still not going to get a basketball scholarship."

Arriving at my ball, we stepped off the distance from the edge of the trap. Some quick math revealed we had two hundred yards to the flag.

"Let's go with the Hook Hotch so we can aim right to take the front bunker out of play," said Herb. "It would be a very hard par out of the bunker with that front left pin. Judging how steeply uphill this is, you need to hit it pretty hard. Take a couple of deep breaths and pretend you know what you're doing."

Following Herb's advice, I took a couple of relaxing breaths, settled into my address position, and hit a solid shot—a little too solid. My ball finished twenty feet above the hole, leaving a treacherously fast putt.

Wiley and Billy Dale elected to gamble, believing they needed to get to six under for a chance to force a playoff. Billy Dale choked a nine-iron, intending to just barely clear the bunker for a makeable uphill birdie putt. His shot looked good in the air but caught the lip of the bunker and trickled back into the bottom. Billy Dale managed a smile. He handed the club back to Wiley, saying, "At least it didn't plug. Let's go up there and see if we can hole it for a three."

"That young man has come a long way today," Herb offered. "I guarantee you, if that had happened yesterday, he would have thrown a fit and blamed Wiley for picking the wrong club."

We walked up to the green, barely able to hear ourselves think as the gallery broke into a loud sustained applause. I started to sense that after four days of viewing me with little more than mild curiosity, the fans were starting to embrace me. This appeared to be especially true of the senior citizens, who made up the majority of the patrons around the green. I suspected they were getting some sort of vicarious fantasy experience from my performance. As I bent to mark my ball, Herb told me to stop. "Better use this," he suggested. He snapped the coin-size medallion off his watch fob and handed it to me. "For luck," he explained.

Billy Dale didn't waste much time. He waded into the bunker, dug his feet into a firm stance, and blasted out. His ball went into the hole on the fly! The place went nuts. Billy Dale appeared too stunned to react. Wiley hugged him and began jumping up and down. His man had just completed an amazing comeback, shooting six under on the back nine to tie for the lead. It looked as if he would at least be in a playoff and might win outright, given the difficulty of my putt. A three-putt from my position would not be unusual.

"Hmm," I whispered after the gallery had quieted. "The medallion was supposed to be good luck for us, not for Billy Dale. Do you think God has changed his mind? Would His purpose be better served if Billy Dale won?"

"The way I have this figured," Herb said, "is that God wants proof of your faith and so is bringing everything in the mission together in this one ultimate nutshell of the whole experience. Either that, or

God just wants this finish to be more memorable so folks won't forget about it for a long, long time. I have faith you're gonna make this putt. The question is, do *you* have faith? The whole world is about to find out right now."

The several thousand patrons were completely silent. The quiet bordered on eerie as I replaced my ball. I put Herb's medallion in my pocket and assumed my address position. The putt was extremely fast. Lagging it close would be akin to putting a ball down a marble staircase with the intent of stopping it on the second step from the bottom.

I muttered a quick prayer, took a relaxing breath, and barely tapped the ball. It took only a few seconds, but it seemed like an eternity as the ball slowly wound its way down the slope. Unable to watch, I closed my eyes and waited. I didn't realize until the gallery exploded what had happened: I had holed it.

I was in shock. Herb seemed happy but not at all surprised. Billy Dale and Wiley came over to congratulate me. They were disappointed but realized they had been part of something very special. None of us wanted to leave the green. However, the tournament wasn't over yet. Either of the remaining players could tie my seven-under mark with an eagle at eighteen.

Rather than head directly to the scorer's desk, Herb and I stood behind the green to witness the approach shots. Scott Thomas played to the green first, hitting a respectable shot ten feet right of the pin. Going for broke, Michael Cameron's shot hit the pin and rebounded back into the bunker.

Herb and I had won the Masters!

EPILOGUE

It has been almost a year since I was escorted to the Butler Cabin for the Green Jacket Ceremony.

Tempting as it was, I didn't do the navy-blue bit. I had a serious message to deliver, and I didn't want to start off sounding like a clown.

The presentation ceremony was a little unusual, to say the least. After the previous year's champion helped me slip into the green jacket, I was expected to say a few words. Everyone in the room, as well as those watching on television, expected to hear me tell a golf story. I told them my story wasn't about golf. It wasn't about me either. It was about them. "My victory today was the culmination of a yearlong mission," I said. "The sole purpose of this victory was to get you to pay attention to the message I'm about to deliver." I proceeded to tell the whole story. I concluded with a summary of the main points. "This is extremely simple. If it weren't, God would not have chosen an aging small-town banker as His messenger. God has given all of us access to the greatest power in the universe. Each of you can do far, far more than you presently think you can. Your lives were never intended to be seemingly endless series of groundhog days. God is always there and always willing to partner with you.

"Meet Him halfway. As with my case, one of the best ways is to change your concept of a day. Trade relatively wasteful late-evening hours for highly productive early-morning hours. Use your newfound morning hours to change your life. Meditate. Pray. Listen. Answers will come. Often, the answer will come in the form of a gut feeling, an inexpressible certainty. Words and labels are very limiting.

"We are at our most profound when we go beyond them to a level of expressionless understanding."

An uncomfortable silence settled over the room. I had caught them flat-footed. The follow-up questions prepared by the interviewers didn't seem very relevant after my little speech. After a few handshakes and awkward congratulations, I left the cabin in search of Herb.

I found him in the parking lot, loading my clubs and other gear into the trunk of the rental car. "How'd it go back there?" he asked.

"I kept it short and sweet," I replied. "Hard to tell what the long-range effect is going to be. It looked to me as if there were mixed reactions. Some of them appeared to almost instantly accept what I was saying as truth, some looked as if they wanted to believe it but needed to think about it, and some looked like they thought I was absolutely nuts."

"Well, you can lead a horse to water. It's not your fault if he falls in and drowns," Herb said, smiling. "Let's head for home. By the way, in case you haven't already figured this out, God and I didn't exactly give you full disclosure. Your mission doesn't end here. You'll be carrying this message for the rest of your life."

"I figured as much. Wouldn't have it any other way."

Life only vaguely resembled my premission routine after I returned home. I received a constant stream of requests to be on talk shows, give lectures, and make other public appearances.

Some well-meaning friends encouraged me to use my newly acquired notoriety to run for office. Our long-term state senator, Gerald Carruthers, had decided not to run again. I had become about the most well-known guy around. My friends thought I would be a lock to win. It took Fletcher about two minutes to talk me out of it. "Joe," he said, shaking his finger in my face, "you are too much of a Boy Scout to make it in politics. They would chew your naïve butt up and spit it out. You are not the type. While our current political system may not prove that the cream rises to the top, it certainly demonstrates that crap floats. Go do something better with your life."

I contacted the Masters Tournament committee and let them know I didn't plan to compete again. But I promised to be there for the Champions Dinner and the Green Jacket Ceremony. My participation in the tournament had served its purpose. I didn't want to take up a spot that could be put to better use.

I haven't had time to play much golf since the April tournament. When I do get a chance to play, it's more often than not a round with my friends. Like Herb suggested, we make up entertaining ways to play each hole. We have a great time, laughing our way around the course with no concern about shooting a score. I am gradually atrophying back to being a contented ten-handicapper.

The last time I saw Herb was two weeks after our return from Augusta. He came into my office with Connell Thomas. Betti was kind enough to bring us coffee as we sat around my desk. "We need to use one of your notaries," Herb explained. "I'm deeding my place over to Connell. He plans to retire from Hemphill next month and wants to use my place for a junior golf camp. Should keep him out of trouble. Tootie and I are leaving in the morning to help that other Joe in Texas. But don't worry—if you need me, I'll know about it and be right there for you. Somehow, I don't think it will ever be necessary."

"I'm working with my board to finalize my retirement plans," I replied. "Before I went to the state banking convention last September, I made some telephone calls to the presidents of two other community banks in neighboring towns. Not surprisingly, they have almost exactly the same problems with the compliance examiners as we have. I arranged for all of us to stay an extra day at the state banking convention to share ideas. Over the ensuing months, we've developed a darn good plan. We've decided to merge, effectively lowering everyone's compliance costs to a third. Our lending cultures and commitments to our communities are very similar. This is a far better scenario for our customers than selling out to a large bank. One of their presidents, Bob Hodges, is fifty years old. He will lead the combined organization. The other guy is my age and plans to retire along with me. We will both hang around as consultants to make sure the transition goes smoothly. This is great for me because it frees time for setting up a series of lectures and meetings to help spread our Masters Mission message. I may even take a shot at writing a book about it."

After Betti notarized the deed, we stood as they prepared to leave. I shook Connell's hand and wished him luck. Herb and I hugged for a long time. Neither of us could come up with words, which was probably a good thing.

True to His word, God has not started any more online chats or sent me any more e-mails. However, I am certain He has stayed in constant communication with me, just as He does with all of us. Every time I experience a burst of inspiration or an occurrence that I used to assume was just a coincidence, I know He is sending me a message. I've gradually learned to be a better listener.

ABOUT THE AUTHOR

 Joe Bullock has been a banker for more than forty years and has managed several institutions. He played golf in college and won several city and regional championships as a young man. He currently resides with his wife and a variety of loveable dogs in Las Cruces, New Mexico.

Lightning Source UK Ltd.
Milton Keynes UK
UKOW05f1144260117
292939UK00001B/100/P